MYSTICS AND MASHED POTATOES

BY

JANIS WALKER

AUTHOR OF

ALLELUIA! A GOSPEL DIARY

Alleluia!
Janis & Terry

Books by Janis Walker

ALLELUIA! A GOSPEL DIARY

FIRST READING: A DIARY

HALLELUJAH! A PSALM RESPONSE DIARY

SECOND READING: A DIARY

A TRIP TO GRACE

SHEPHERDS

MYSTERY!

MYSTICS AND MASHED POTATOES

MYSTICS AND MASHED POTATOES

BY

JANIS WALKER

PALLIUM PRESS

Scripture quotations marked NRSV are from The New Revised Standard Version Bible, copyright 1989, Division of Christian Education of the National Council of Churches of Christ in the United States of America.

Scripture quotations marked KJV are from the The King James Version of the Bible.

Every effort has been made to insure accuracy of text and quotations, and any errors or omissions brought to our attention will be corrected in future editions.

FIRST PRINTING 2016

Pallium Press, P.O. Box 60910, Palo Alto, CA 94306-0910
We regret that Pallium Press cannot accept or return unsolicited manuscripts.

Check for new titles by Janis Walker at www.palliumpress.com

Pallium Press books are available at www.Amazon.com, www.BarnesandNoble.com, or at your favorite local independent bookstore.

cover photo: Terry Walker
cover design: Janis Walker

Copyright © 2016 by Janis Walker

Printed in the United States of America.

ISBN 978-0-9826883-7-3

for

The St. Patrick's Seminary Class of 1991

and

in memory of Father Mark Catalana, Class of 1991

"Blessed are the pure in heart, for they will see God."
Matthew 5, 8

Acknowledgements

Thank you to Terry, Christopher, and to all the "Mystics" in my life who have been my mentors, inspiring me to look to heaven and to all the "Potatoes" who have helped me to keep my feet on the ground and to fulfill my mission

Over the years I've enjoyed the many friends the Lord has brought across my path to share the journey Home. We have prayed together, laughed together, shared times of sorrow, chatted over coffee, and plotted ways we could assist the Lord in running the universe. Regarding the latter, the Lord usually says, "Thank you for sharing. Just finish your cappuccino; it's getting cold."

With one particular friend, an artistic soul, I met once for coffee at a golf course, while her high school son (pre-driver's license) took golf lessons. The view of the golf course was lovely, but the coffee was dreadful! Noticing the menu and the high price for this atrocious coffee, my friend remarked, "Just think, Janis, for 15 cents more, we could have mashed potatoes!" Since this particular friend is a mystic, as well as a very practical person, I vowed one day to jot down a few essays under the title <u>Mystics and Mashed Potatoes</u>.

Since that time, her son has a driver's license, played soccer, graduated from high school and college, is married, and has children. We still talk and pray together -- at places with much better coffee!

A.M.D.G.

21 November 2015

The Presentation of the Blessed Virgin Mary

MACARONI IN THE MONASTERY

Many years ago, long before I studied in the seminary, I discovered a beautiful monastery in a nearby town. It is located on a busy street with lots of noise and traffic.

Once inside the large, beautiful chapel, the outside noise does not matter that much. There are candles burning, sunlight pouring through the stained-glass windows, and a deep sense of peace. The chapel is kept open all day. Outside there are lovely gardens.

Sometimes, at the back of the chapel, people leave little holy cards or other "freebies." Once, I glanced across the aisle and saw a small card, about the size of a recipe card. Sure enough, it was a recipe card, a card from a nearby grocery store with a recipe for Pasta and Shrimp Primavera.

Why not? Jesus ministered to the whole person -- body, soul, and spirit. The kind person who left a pasta recipe in the monastery was simply continuing this practical ministry.

Part 1   CHERITH

The reflections in the "Cherith" section come from 1986-1991, my years at St. Patrick's Seminary. I was an Episcopalian at the time and was very grateful for the seminary's ecumenical generosity in allowing me to come and study.

Since the seminary is only two or so miles from our home, I could care for my family and also study for my Master's in Theology degree without a long commute time. I was very blessed and remain very grateful.

My years at St. Patrick's Seminary were my "Cherith" years. Cherith was the name of the brook, east of the Jordan River, where the prophet Elijah was sheltered for a time and fed by the "ravens." (1Kings 17)

Good Morning, Sister

One of my first mornings at St. Patrick's, I was walking down the C wing. One of the men who worked in Buildings and Grounds smiled and said, very respectfully, "Good morning, Sister."

I did a double-take, trying to decide how to respond. He must have thought I was a nun.

What would a nun say? I did not grow up Catholic and knew nothing about nuns.

My junior year college roommate, Johanna, was Catholic. She knew about nuns, but I knew nothing.

Did I say, "I am married and have a son?"

I just smiled and said, "Hi!"

Purified Priests and Papist Parakeets

I believe it was spring of 1987 when I took the course, "Prophets" from Fr. Michael Guinan, a very distinguished Scripture scholar. Fr. Guinan, a Franciscan priest and professor at the Franciscan School of Theology in Berkeley, commuted over to St. Patrick's to teach this course.

I asked Fr. Guinan to suggest a topic for my term paper. He suggested writing a paper tracing and analyzing the various times in the Hebrew scriptures where the prophets criticize the priests for not living up to their sacred calling.

Writing this paper was very therapeutic for me personally as well as academically fascinating. The title was "Purify the Priests," based on the third chapter of Malachi.

At that time, Christopher kept parakeets as pets, usually two at a time in a large cage in our sunny dining room. Sometimes the birds were allowed out of their cage.

With the large glass windows in our home, occasionally there would be a tragedy, resulting yet another little cross in the Arboretum on the Stanford campus. Another little bird committed to God's eternal care.

Knowing that Fr. Guinan was a Franciscan priest, I thought it would be wise to have the current two little birds blessed. I took the cage up to the seminary for my class lecture. Remember, St. Francis also preached to the birds!

After class, we had a little processional to the holy water font outside the seminary chapel. Fr. Guinan duly blessed the birdies and I took them home. Christopher was very impressed with this and said, "Wow, now I have papist parakeets!"

Nun Cards

Many times during my years of study in the seminary, I had the joy of attending ordinations to the deaconate and to the priesthood. At an ordination in Sacramento, at Blessed Sacrament Cathedral, I remember sitting near an elderly lady who was quietly translating the ordination rite into Latin. She became very animated, returned to English, and asked, "Did he get de oil yet?"

At the ordination of the Class of 1991, at St. Joseph's Cathedral in San Jose, I proudly carried along cards for the newly ordained priests. There were tables at the reception for cards and gifts.

Part way through the reception, one of the new priests from the Class of 1991 came up to me, laughing. "Janis," he said, "These cards are for nuns!"

I was baffled. "How can that be? The cards talk about vows and priests make vows."

He kept laughing, saying, "Trust me on this. These are nun cards." Oh well, I was not a Catholic back then. I didn't know.

A Mitre in Your Hope Chest?

A group of seminarians was asked by a professor about their hope for their future. Did they see themselves as future leaders? Did they see themselves as obscure servants?

The place of greatest joy and fulfillment may not be where we think it is. The greatest place of contentment is abiding close to Jesus and following him into the part of the vineyard assigned to us.

The Pope and the Cheerleader

Back in seminary days, one particular second year seminarian, now a distinguished priest, had an uncanny gift of imitating the gestures of Pope John Paul II.

He would hold up his arms, nod and smile in a most cherubic, beneficent manner. At his ordination to the priesthood, while congratulating him at the door of the church, someone asked him to do his famous imitation of the Holy Father. He graciously declined.

The "cheerleader" was another story. Another of the seminarians, a gifted musician, also had a gift of imitation.

One day in the hallway, he was imitating a cheerleader from a movie. The cheer went something like, "U-G-L-Y, you ain't got no alibi! You is UGLY!"   Years later, upon request, he obligingly repeated the cheer.

This was all done in good humor. Even Pope John Paul II, now a saint, was said to have had an uncanny gift at doing impersonations.

Phone Call from Rome

Poor Terry! I called him in California to tell him about some challenging circumstances in Rome.

It was October, 1989, the fall of my fourth year in the seminary. I was on a pilgrimage organized by the archdiocese, to Medjugorje and Rome.

The permanent deacon and his wife, who were in our group, were staying in the room next door to my room in the hotel in Rome. I remembered something about the deacon's wife having to have ear plugs. Now I knew why! The wonderful deacon was also a world-class snorer. I just could not sleep.

Then, I could not make the toilet stop running. The handle was up on the wall. European plumbing was beyond me.

I phoned Terry, in California, for advice! I don't remember what time it was in California, but Terry was very gracious. He told me what to do to the toilet to make it stop running.

Then he advised going to the front desk of the hotel and trying to arrange for another room. This I did, with much arm-waving and trying to figure out how to convey "snoring" in Italian.

The last couple of days of our time in Rome were wonderful. While in the Vatican, the deacon and his wife arranged for us to have a day in Assisi. Then it was time to go home. I arrived in San Francisco shortly after the earthquake, but that is another story.

Sallie, Grace, and Jack

It was a really busy week-end in March, 1990. After Friday classes in the seminary, Terry took me to the airport so I could fly to Sallie's parish out of state for a week-end of ministry. Sallie is a dear clergy friend who, at that time, was rector of a beautiful Episcopal church, called Grace.

On Saturday, I gave a Lenten "Quiet Day" (Day of Recollection) at Sallie's church, Grace Church, preached at both the 8:00 am and 10 am Holy Eucharist services on Sunday at Grace, and then flew back.

In the airport, I saw a NEW YORKER magazine with a pastel painting of a jack-in-the box. I had often felt like "Jack." Sometimes I had to stay in the box in the darkness and trust that I was serving God with my prayers, studies, waiting, and writing. Sometimes, I was invited to come out of the box and to minister in a more visible way. All that matters is to serve the Lord as the Lord is leads.

The Seminary and the Sidewalk

One of the most rewarding aspects of my time in the seminary was when I would go to a nearby city to pray the rosary and to work with several Catholic friends in an ecumenical ministry. We went literally to the people, on the "sidewalk," to offer what assistance we could in their crisis situation.

There was a flight attendant, an artist, an attorney, a physicist, and several others in this ministry. I learned so much from them and how they practiced their Catholic faith. Without ever "preaching" to me, their vibrant practice of their Catholic faith impressed me deeply long before I became a Catholic myself.

Taco Trucks and Lap Swimming

Another wonderful memory of seminary days was the year of taco trucks and lap swimming. A YMCA in a nearby city had a special offer, a one year membership for only $99!

This was great on days my classes ended early. I could drive away from the seminary, stop at one of the handy taco trucks on the way for a delicious ninety cent taco, go swim it off at the Y, and still get back home to be with Christopher after he got out of school.

Translations of "Live in Berkeley" and "Monastery"

Many years ago, before I entered St. Patrick's Seminary, I was perplexed about where we would live if I ever went to seminary. Our family lived in Silicon Valley and the seminary I had planned to enter was in Berkeley.

I kept wondering how we could "live in Berkeley." It just did not seem feasible with Terry's work and with Christopher's school right here in Silicon Valley.

Perhaps I would not be able to enter seminary after all in the fall of 1986. That was a summer of praying for guidance.

As it turned out, I did live near the seminary. Very near. Two and a half miles away from Christopher's school!

What happened? In God's providence, the doors closed on my entering the seminary in Berkeley and opened to my entering, even though I was not yet a Catholic, the beautiful seminary, St. Patrick's, in Menlo Park.

Years later, the word "monastery" kept popping up as I prayed. Monastery? What in the world? I didn't grow up Catholic.

What God was trying to get across to me was very simple. The monastery near the seminary was to become a place of learning to pray in a new way. I was learning to be quiet.

In addition to my involvement in ecumenical prayer group ministry, wonderful though it was over many years, I was also being called to pray in another way. Silence. Solitude. Adoration.

Sometimes it takes awhile to receive God's translations. God is always inviting us into a new realm of wonder and growth.

Here endeth the Cherith stories for now.

Part 2 THE GALILEE and JERUSALEM

These are simple reflections on simple everyday situations. Some are humorous. Others are more serious. They all have to do with my relationship with God. They are not in any precise chronological order.

Sarah Goes to Seminary (Again)

Easter Wednesday, 2002. For the last time I drove Sarah, my faithful friend and road companion, a 1979 Olds Cutlass, to St. Patrick's Seminary.

A seminarian needed a car and Sarah, although old, was still mechanically very sound. I was so happy she would be appreciated and would help a future priest.

Before leaving home, I anointed Sarah with blessed oil from the Jesuit Retreat House and asked Terry to say a prayer. At the seminary, Fr. Bob Gavin and a seminarian also prayed.

Why carry on so about a piece of moving metal? Because Sarah and I go back a long time.

She wasn't always called Sarah. She came to our family in 1980, as a used car. Christopher was five years old and I still have a picture of him, in his little English schoolboy grey shorts and sweaters, with Sarah in the background. There's another picture of little Christopher in his Superman outfit, with Sarah in the background.

Sarah first went to another seminary in the fall of 1985. On Monday evenings I gritted my teeth and plunged into a once a week three hour class in New Testament Greek, taught by the compassionate Rev. Kent Meads at the Fuller Seminary Extension in Menlo Park.

I made Mondays "Picnic Night "at home, often serving a rotisserie chicken from the JJ&F Market. Easy cooking before I clutched my vocabulary cards, my Greek New Testament, and Exegetical Fallacies, and headed out the door.

In the fall of 1986, by divine providence, I began my studies at St. Patrick's Seminary. At that time I was not a Roman Catholic and believed I would be attending a seminary in Berkeley. When that was not possible, I prayed for guidance all summer. Every time I prayed for guidance, the Holy Spirit would say, "Call St. Patrick's Seminary." "ST PATRICK'S !!? They're CATHOLIC!" The Holy Spirit persisted and one day that summer I called St. Patrick's. The kind person who answered the phone, sensing my terror, asked me to come and talk with the acting Academic Dean. St. Patrick's sheltered me for five fruitful years of study.

In his school years, Christopher took many trips with Sarah. To and from school, from kindergarten on, when he did not take his bicycle. Mid-week trips with friends to Coyote Hills to fly his remote control gliders. Soccer practice. Piano lessons. Trumpet lessons. Scout meetings. One summer, he was a NASA intern. Terry would drive him there in the station wagon in the morning and I would pick him up in the late afternoon. As a hungry teenager, he liked to stop at Mexican restaurants or Hong Kong bakery for huge "snacks" on the way home!

From 1993-94, Sarah and I went to the bus stop at Waverley and Homer for me to catch the Dumbarton Express to Union City. From there I caught the BART to Berkeley for a year's study at another seminary. I would leave Sarah in the parking lot across from St. Thomas Aquinas Church at about 7:15 a.m. Across the street I could see the holy water font at St. Thomas and I longed to be there. One morning, I could not bear it so I went to Mass and still was able, barely, to catch the bus.

During that same year, Sarah and I also went to East Palo Alto and then across the Dumbarton Bridge to a city in the East Bay where I served as a Field Ed. seminarian in an Episcopal church. On Sundays, Terry and I went there together. I preached on occasion, met with the Confirmation class, and gave Advent and Lenten Days of Recollection.

In the summer of 1994, Sarah and I went to the hospitals where I completed my Clinical Pastoral Education in the Stanford program.

Our group was at the VA location. We also made treks for didactics at the main hospital at Stanford, the Stanford Children's Hospital, and to the Menlo Park VA. The time at the Children's Hospital was very moving. We saw the premature babies and the room with the tiny baptismal garments for emergency baptisms.

Before going to the VA, I drove up the hill to early Mass at the Immaculate Heart Monastery of the Poor Clares and then back down the hill just in time!

Since 1994, Sarah and I have traveled to many ecumenical prayer groups. We've traveled to Mass, met friends for tea, gone to the market, gone to the Palo Alto Y for lap swimming.

Many years of traveling with Sarah. Years associated with family, friends, and ministry.

The name "Sarah" emerged years ago after considering the Sarah of Genesis and her long wait for the promise of Isaac to be fulfilled. Abraham, too, believed, although there seemed to be no reason to believe, that God's promise to him would be fulfilled (Romans 4, 18). The promise was fulfilled with the birth of Isaac. "Sarah then said, 'God hath made me to laugh, so that all who hear will laugh with me (Genesis 21, 6 KJV)."

Doughnuts and an Axe Murder

I was on the way to the Jesuit Retreat House for a Day of Recollection. It was Ash Wednesday, a day for serious reflection and prayer.

On the way, I passed a doughnut shop and kept driving. Doughnuts, two kinds in particular, used to exert a powerful influence over me!

Congratulating myself that I had resisted the doughnut temptation, I proceeded to the retreat house. Only a few blocks from the doughnut shop, I realized with a pounding heart and with a terrible intensity that, although it was relatively easy to resist a doughnut, it was not so easy to resist harboring angry thoughts.

Old hurts tend to surface, often at unexpected times, as we are endeavoring to draw closer to God. The enemy of our souls loves to torment us.

Yes, it is true that Jesus said that not only murderers will face God's judgment, but also that being angry and insulting others will bring God's judgment (Matthew 5, 21-22). It is also true that God forgives us in the same way that we forgive others (Matthew 6, 12).

God alone can enter the recesses of our hearts and ease the anger that could lead to the kind of rage that could lead to murder. We are dependent of God's grace and mercy at all times. God sees all injustices. God will take care of what concerns us.

Having this flash of insight about myself was a good and healthy way to begin Lent. Better than doughnuts.

Marmalade in the AFTERNOON?!

Many years ago, on our first trip to England, we decided to enjoy afternoon tea in a well-known large department store in London. I did not know the unwritten code about marmalade!

Marmalade was usually offered at breakfast, but not later. Asking for marmalade with the scones brought a shocked expression from the server.

"Marmalade in the afternoon?!" she inquired with a look of shocked disapproval. Strawberry jam, we were informed, was the correct choice.

What happens to us in this life if we do things differently? What happens if we are late bloomers or if we blossom early?

To be true to God and true to ourselves, we have to be willing to be different. Not in an ostentatious way. Not to draw attention to ourselves.

Rather, we need to learn to breathe and live in the God-space we have been given and to do things in the God-time we have been assigned. Maybe marmalade in the afternoon is not so shocking, after all!

This Could Be the Start of Something Feline

In the summer of 1986, when Christopher was eleven, we had a wonderful three weeks in England. Terry was asked to spend a week as lecturer at a physics lab near Oxford. We were given a beautiful two-story house to live in for three whole weeks, while the owners were in Wales.

On the first morning in England, Terry drove off to the lab. Christopher and I were "home," getting acquainted with our new surroundings, which included a view of meadows and sheep.

Feeling very drowsy and jet-lagged, I decided to take a little nap in one of the bedrooms. I was startled to awaken with a sense of pressure on my chest and with two eyes staring into mine.

Tomkins! Tomkins, the family cat, had come to claim his own favorite spot for a nap! I was unknowingly napping on his own favorite morning nap place.

This was the start of our family's association with cats. Neither Terry or I had grown up with cats. Christopher's pets, since second grade, had been parakeets, beginning with Mike and Monica.

Christopher and Tomkins hit it off from the start. The fat old marmalade cat had to relinquish all his ideas of the easy life, while the kid from California was around! There were many adventures all over the house and the back garden. which included a pond and greenhouse.

Some days, while Terry was at the lab, Christopher and I would take the footpath, about a mile and three quarters, to the next village, Wantage. We would walk around a bit, shop for groceries at Waitrose, and catch the county bus, the "Whizzer" back to our village of Letcombe Regis. Tompkins was waiting for us.

After Terry had completed his week's work at the lab, we still had two delightful weeks to travel and explore this corner of England. We took the "fast" train into London and many motor jaunts into the countryside. One evening, we were driving back, when we noticed a sign that a French boys' choir would be performing that evening in a village not too far away.

This was a dilemma! One of our duties at the house was, of course, to feed Tomkins. If we went to the concert and returned home late, would Tomkins starve to death? Not being used to cats, we decided against the concert, in deference to our furry friend.

After returning to America, I continued to miss Tomkins. A store downtown selling stuffed toy animals had a cat that looked just like Tomkins.

Years passed. Christopher was now fifteen. One October afternoon, I was sitting in the back garden under the palm tree, reading. It was a warm day and I took the parakeets in their large cage with me into the garden.

MEOW! Looking up hastily from my book, I saw a huge marmalade cat. No, it couldn't be Tomkins!

Where did this creature come from? Rushing the birds back inside to safety, I continued to wonder.

Christopher came home from high school, spotted the cat, and asked, "Mom, can we feed him?" The cat, although large, did act a little pathetic. I went to the pet store and came back with a few sample sacks of dry food. Somehow, I picked up the wrong samples. This was dog food, not cat food. Oh, well, we offered it anyway to our visitor. He seemed puzzled, but ate it.

The cat kept coming back. A friend said, "Janis, this is not a starving stray cat. It belongs somewhere."

Since the cat came to us around the time of the feast of St. Francis, we decided to name him "Francis." We had a tag made with our phone numbers, so the "real" owners could contact us.

Within a day, the phone rang. The cat, whose name was "Biff" lived in the next block. Terry returned him to his home.

Still, he continued to come to our back garden. Every evening, Terry returned him.

Finally, his owners said, "We have two children and several pets, including a dog named Spike. Why don't you keep Biff?"

They were very gracious and generous. They told us that Biff was a neutered male, about five years old.

Since I had gotten used to calling him Francis, I decided to keep that name. Somehow I could not call this gentle creature "Biff."

Francis is now a mellow, older gentleman cat in excellent health. Just like Tomkins, he has his favorite places, usually Christopher's bed, for his morning naps in the sunshine.

Cats continued to be part of Christopher's life. While at Caltech studying physics, he and his friends adopted several kittens. The Dabney

House cats were lovingly cared for by the students. Three became Christopher's own cats. The little kitten, Corwin, was tragically killed in traffic and was buried with a little cross. Toto and Negri continued to live with Christopher, off campus, for years.

Tomkins really started something!

The Rose Chasuble

This happened many years ago on Sunday, the third Sunday in Advent. For some reason, it was very important to me that Sunday, Gaudete Sunday, to see the rose vestments. We were out of town, I believe.

Violet was the color of the vestments at the Mass we attended that morning. Maybe that church did not have rose vestments.

We drove to a couple of other churches to spy out the vestments. No rose vestments there. I had a curious sense of sadness and loss.

Goats at the Damascus Gate

Jerusalem! I'm fortunate to have gotten out of that scrape!

In April, 1985, I was in Jerusalem with a group of Episcopalians at St. George's Anglican College. The late Rev. Brad Hall, Rector of St. Margaret's, Palm Desert, was our director

We were there for two weeks of study, lectures, worship, and travel.There was an Australian Anglican monk named Gilbert, who lectured at the college and made the most wonderful chutney. Gilbert also seriously cautioned us to drink enough water on our desert treks.

We were told that it was interesting to go to the Damascus Gate, on Friday morning, to see the goat market. So, my tall blonde roommate, Linda, and I proceeded very early that Friday to see the goats.

We stopped first for a little nourishment. We purchased bread from a street vendor and sprinkled the bread with aromatic herbs. Delicious!

Then we walked into the market among the goats. After a few minutes, Linda quietly spoke to me, She had noticed that Brad, was outside the goat market, motioning in a rather stunned way, for us to leave.

We found out later that it was absolutely taboo, a real cultural no-no for women to be in the goat market. Standing from afar and looking at the goats, yes. Walking among the goats, no! Gilbert was horrified.

We felt very mortified. but we didn't know. It was one of those cultural things we simply did not know.

Confessional Door

Well, the sign said to use the "other" door! I walked to a confessional box and seeing the sign, used the "other" door.

There sat the priest! I guess I was still too new a Catholic to realize that the "other" door meant the door on the other side, not the middle door. I stammered, "I am sorry, Father, " and then found the correct "other" door.

Blow-dry Novenas

As a new Catholic, I sometimes prayed novenas as I dried my hair with a blow drier. After telling a cradle Catholic about this, I decided it was better not to tell others about my unusual ways of praying. The Lord doesn't mind, I don't think, but sometimes others do.

Taking St. Joseph Hostage

Such a simple request, or so I thought. John, my brother in Texas, was trying to sell our late mother's house in February, a slow time.

15

Then I remembered something about asking the intercession of St. Joseph. Years ago, in a bookstore, I had seen a statue of St. Joseph to put in the yard if you wanted to sell your house. So, I phoned a nearby Catholic book store to see about this.

"Do you have any statues of St. Joseph?" I asked. "How tall you want?" inquired the saleswoman. "Well, not very tall," I nervously replied, envisioning a thirty foot statue.

Eventually, I got her to tell me that the smallest size was three inches tall. Relieved, I asked my husband to go buy the statue, while I ran other Saturday errands.

He returned home with the little plastic statue and with quite a story. The saleswoman demanded of him, "You going to sell a house! Do NOT bury this statue. You can't take St. Joseph hostage."

She went on and on. The last thing she said as Terry paid for the statue and left was, "Be sure and don't bury St. Joseph."

At first I was amused and then irritated. After all, she was there to sell books and other products, not to harangue the customers. Still, she showed the courage of her convictions.

Actually it does not seem very respectful to bury a statue. What I had in mind was to place the little statue discreetly under a bush in Mother's garden.

So I mailed the statue to Karl, Mother's Catholic neighbor, carefully warning him not to bury St. Joseph. Karl and his wife, Susan, had been so kind and had, as I requested, taken Mother's statue of the Blessed Virgin Mary, to their garden to place among the tomato plants.

The Nonstick Chalice (March 3, 2002)

Many mornings I pray "The Prayer of the Chalice." This prayer by Frances Nuttall from England was handed out at an ecumenical conference I attended in the 1970's.

16

The scripture reference given was the last part of Nehemiah 1,11 KJV, "For I was the king's cupbearer."

This prayer has been with me for many years. I prayed it before I served as chalice bearer as a Episcopalian and continue to pray it as a Catholic.

Something happened to me today. As I was praying the Prayer of the Chalice, I realized that I have been like a non-stick chalice.

You know those skillets that are great for cooking because they are coated? The contents never really soak into the skillet.

That's good for skillets, but it hasn't been good for me. Drained and depleted, I need to be filled again in order to give to others. I need the Holy Spirit to permeate every fiber of my being before I can give again.

Hold the Peace

Last night, we attended a crowded Maundy Thursday service at a nearby church. The woman sitting next to me seemed very devout and very intent on the liturgy.

Imagine my surprise, when, at the Peace, she held her hands together and refused to share the Peace. She said, "I don't shake."

"I don't shake?!" I was reminded of two of my culinary foibles. I enjoy all the rich, gooey filling of pecan pie, although I cannot, or should not, eat the pecans. "I'd like a piece of pecan pie - hold the pecans."

Years ago, I was trying to cut back on carbohydrates. At a fast food hamburger place, I said, "I'd like a hamburger - hold the bread." The mystified, but obliging cashier presented me with the insides of a hamburger in one those little styrofoam boxes.

Sometimes it is wise to "hold your peace" and to remain silent. But to "hold the peace" during the liturgy baffles me. To refuse to offer

17

the peace of Christ baffles me.

I don't think we, as Christ's Body on this earth, can be complete without expressing his peace to one another, in one way or another. But, as my friend Bee used to say, "That is only my opinion."

Of Honor and Estate Sales

In late summer, we were staying at the old inn in Vermont we love so much. It is in a tiny, peaceful village.

Our morning routine is for me to have early morning coffee on the porch, while Terry gets ready for breakfast. Then he crosses the street from our cottage and we go in to breakfast together in the dining room of the inn. The red flannel hash, topped with perfectly poached eggs, was beyond wonderful!

So, this particular morning, I was enjoying the sunshine, the coffee, and the bright scarlet red geraniums and fragrant white petunias on the porch.

Four people were crossing the street (it's a little street) to come over for breakfast. We began to chat.

The older couple were from California and the younger couple were their daughter and son-in-law from the East coast. When asked where we were from in California, I answered.

Then, when Terry crossed the street, the older couple became quite animated. "There he is! There's that man!"

What in the world? Well, it really is a small world.

It turned out that Terry had gone to an estate sale in our town some time back. At the estate sale, there were a lot of electronic items, etc. that he found very interesting. He purchased a number of items. Upon returning home, however, he began to think about it and decided that the people running the sale really should have charged more.

So, he went back and insisted on paying more! Trust me, that sort of thing just does not happen around here.

The people at the sale were so amazed. As it turned out, they were the people closing the estate of the wife's father. They were the very people running the estate sale.

So, when they saw him at the inn in Vermont, all they could say was, "There's that man!" A man of honor.

Christ the King, Sunday, November 25, 2001

On this particular day, when we are gripped with the uncertainties of war, we are grateful that it is the time in the Church year to ponder the sovereignty of Christ. It is the crucified Lamb of God who is our King.

The reading in the Book of Second Samuel prepares us for the kingship of Christ by reminding us of the kingship of David. David, the shepherd lad, was chosen by God to be King of Israel.

God told David, "It is you who shall be shepherd of my people Israel, you who shall be ruler over Israel (2 Samuel 5, 2b)." Shepherd. Ruler.

Psalm 122, in which we are instructed to pray for the peace of Jerusalem, also speaks of judgment seats or thrones. David, as king, would judge his people, as well as serve as their shepherd and commander.

St. Paul, writing to the Colossian church, used graphic language to describe our King. Jesus Christ is the visible image of God. If you take a snapshot of God, the picture is going to look like Jesus!

God the Father took the initiative to rescue us, to deliver us out of darkness and to transfer us to the kingdom of Jesus, his Son. In this kingdom, we are offered redemption and the forgiveness of all of our sins.

God bought us back. The price was the Blood of his only Son,

Jesus, on the Cross.

Why would a King be on Cross? How would a King who had consented to be a ransom, conduct himself nailed to a Cross?

The Gospel of Luke tells us that Jesus was "sneered at," "jeered at," and "reviled." Above his Cross was the mocking inscription, "This is the King of the Jews."

Jesus, the innocent Lamb, reached out with his shepherd's heart to the repentant thief. "Truly I tell you, today you will be with me in Paradise (Luke 23, 43 NRSV)."

On this Sunday of Christ the King, what can we take with us back into our scary world of terrorism and, what a Jesuit priest and English professor accidentally referred to as "the threat of Xerox?"

What can we take back with us into our world? The correct question is, "Who can we take back with us into our world?"

We receive Jesus, Body and Blood, Soul and Divinity, and we take Jesus with us back into our world. Alleluia!

Mother's Mascara

Mascara?!

As Judy, my sister told me, our mother was in the hospital's emergency room and she was asking for her mascara.

Actually, later, looking back on Mother's hard life, I think it was rather healthy that she was asking for mascara. It was a sign that she still cared about life.

When I visited her in the hospital in Texas, she asked me to go to her home and bring back the cake mascara.

Cake? I thought mascara came in little wands. To Mother,

however, the best mascara came in little cakes, which you applied by swishing a little brush across the mascara and then applying.

Mother and the Monsignor

The last few years of her life, Mother could not get out to her Methodist church, and so she discovered a church service on television that she really enjoyed. It was broadcast from the town where she had grown up, about thirty miles away.

The service was Sunday Mass at the Cathedral with a Monsignor presiding. He was from Ireland and had a wonderful sense of humor. Once, in the middle of a terribly hot Texas summer, he said he would like to be a little boy again in Ireland, rolling down the snowy hillside in his pajamas! Mother thought that was just so funny. "Imagine Monsignor in the snow in his pajamas!"

After Mother was gone, I wanted to talk with Monsignor. After a few long-distance phone calls, I did locate him and told him how much the television Mass had meant to Mother. He was wonderfully understanding and told me Mother was fine. So, now, Mother, I think he's my Monsignor, too.

Mother and Our Lady of Fatima

My sister Judy, who worked on the Princess Cruise Line, had been in Portugal and brought back a statue of Our Lady of Fatima for Mother.

Mother really liked the statue and called her "Fatima." Judy said, "No, Mother, her name is Our Lady of Fatima."

Mother disagreed, saying, "Her name is FATIMA! It says so right there on the statue!"

BONJOUR and a "Dew Kiss"

Jacqueline, my elegant friend from college days in Texas, had done it again! She surprised me with an unexpected little package in the mail.

There was a lovely "Bonjour" plaque for the front porch and there was a hand lotion called "Dew Kiss." I needed some cheering up that day and "Bonjour" and a "kiss" really helped.

Three Camellias

Today was a cold, grey, dreary, drizzly day. I wasn't feeling well and almost did not go to Prayer Group. Arriving late, I began to soak up the healing presence of the Lord and of the other members of the group.

We were definitely weary warriors, prayer warriors, today. Only four of us could attend. So many prayer concerns.

As we prayed, I began to sense the Lord strengthening me. I asked him to come and heal my weary sisters in Christ.

As always, we ended the prayer group with a special blessing. We stood in our little circle and prayed over one another. "May the peace and the love of the Lord be with you and with your family." Slight variations, but always prayer from the heart.

We were all going to noon Mass in a nearby parish. I knew I had to move along fast to get a few things done first. After an errand, I stopped at home.

Time was getting closer to Mass, but I so wanted to give pink camellias from my garden to the three faithful prayer warriors. With all the rain, I dreaded stomping through the mud to get to the camellias.

Walking out on the deck, I noticed camellias blooming where they had never bloomed. There were camellias, three perfect pink camellias, right up close by the deck! All I had to do was to walk over and cut them.

The camellia recipients were surprised and grateful! The real joy was in knowing the Lord had provided this tangible evidence of his love.

Detour or Express Highway?

"The road to resolution lies by doubt: The next way home's the shortest way about (from an epigram of Francis Quarles)."

Today is Ash Wednesday, February 13, 2002. I was reminded that it is very important to ask the Lord to close doors as well as to open doors in our lives. Proverbs 16, 9 tells of the Lord directing our steps.

In 1986, I thought that going to a Catholic seminary was a detour. Now I see that it was God's way of directing my steps on the journey Home. The longest way round was truly the shortest way home.

"For a day in your courts is better than a thousand elsewhere. I would rather be a doorkeeper in the house of my God than to live in the tents of wickedness. For the LORD God is a sun and a shield; he bestows favor and honor. No good thing does the LORD withhold from those who walk uprightly (Psalm 84, 10-11 NRSV)."

Meeting Joseph Again

What was it like when Jesus returned Home to heaven to his Abba, his heavenly Father, mission accomplished? It must the reunion of all reunions!

Joseph. I have also wondered what it was like when Jesus met Joseph again.

Joseph had been his "abba" as an infant, little boy, and maybe as a teenager. We don't know for sure when Joseph died. Again, as with his blessed Mother Mary, it must have been a joyful reunion.

No More Hoops

Years ago, I was making a retreat in another city. The director of the retreat was an abbot of a Benedictine monastery.

I described to the abbot my travails in a previous ministry experience. The use and misuse of such words as "discernment" and "process" were discussed.

The most healing words the abbot spoke to me were words about "hoops" Not basketball hoops, either!

He said, "Janis, no more hoops." Beautiful words which the Lord used to heal me.

I would one day be where the Lord wanted me to be. The Lord would take me there.

Whose Values Are They, Anyway?

After Mass today, I decided to attempt a couple of errands. I was amazed to see a parking place by a fashionable little shop downtown. I had heard of this shop, but had never gone there.

A parking place in this town is almost a form of divine guidance! So, I parked and went into the little boutique, clad in my denim jumper and running shoes. Not exactly dressed for success, but dressed to accommodate a foot problem.

I tried not to gasp as I saw the prices. A linen blazer that looked nice was nearly $500! The last blazer I had bought cost $29.95 at a bargain store. Still, I thought I'd try it on. I laughingly said, "This jacket looks lovely. I'm not exactly dressed in something it would go with, though."

Bad idea to say that. With some people, being honest is an invitation to rudeness.

The sales lady, looking at me with definite disapproval, said, "You certainly are not." I tried it on anyway, returned it to the rack, smiled, said, "Thank you," and left.

As a long-term struggler with oversensitivity, I felt snubbed. Then I thought, "I have just come from Mass, where I have received the

Precious Body and Blood of Jesus." Who cares what anyone else thinks of the way I dress?"

Living in this incredibly competitive, materialistic culture, it is so easy to take our eyes off Jesus. As my "wisdom consultant" friend advised, "Put your eyes back in your own head."

Ministry 101

Mark 3. The Gospel of Mark, Chapter 3. Read it, study it, pray over it, and you will have a blueprint for ministry.

The Dog Ate the Rosary

You've heard about the prophet Ezekiel eating the scroll (Ezekiel 3, 1-4), the prophet Jeremiah devouring God's words (Jeremiah 15,16), and John swallowing the scroll (Revelation 10, 8-11). Now you're going to hear about the Word-eating dog!

Years ago at the Jesuit Retreat Center bookstore, I saw a little book called The Scriptural Rosary. It was tiny and easy to read as one prayed the rosary. It gave the scriptural references for the joyful, sorrowful, and glorious mysteries in the life of Jesus. This little book was published before the addition of the luminous mysteries.

I bought the book and gave it to my friend, Barbara. She is a Catholic with some Baptists in her family, so I thought this combination of Bible and rosary would be just the gift.

Barbara enjoyed it and so did her dog Abby. Abby ate the book!

Hamburger Hacienda

Today, after Prayer Group, I drove one of the members to her home and then ran a few errands. Stopping at a drive-through hamburger place, I decided to drive down the neighborhood street, park the car, and have my $1.07 bargain meal, complete with iced water and a slice of lemon!

Driving down the street, I noticed a Spanish style house, complete with a shade tree by the street and a fountain. After parking under the tree and turning off the ignition, I heard music. Apparently the "hacienda," which is a private home as far as I can tell, had music piped outside. It was a station which played old favorites, such as "Georgia" and "Roses and Lollipops." A very restful, yet classy, lunch.

Within the Hour

On this hot July day in 2002, I realized I had to put into practice something I've preached to myself. For some time, I've noticed that if I don't do certain things, such as writing a special letter, etc. within an hour of the inspiration, the energy fades.

I start procrastinating and say, "Well, I'll do it later." Later sometimes never arrives.

Today, I learned of the death of Mildred Wirt Benson, the "real" person who wrote many of the Nancy Drew books, under the pen name of Carolyn Keene. She was ninety-six and worked at her newspaper job right up until the afternoon she was taken to the hospital.

Earlier this year, in January, I had read about this remarkable woman and had "meant" to write her a note saying my own "thank you" for all the enjoyment the Nancy Drew books have brought me. I never wrote the note.

Understandably we cannot possibly do all the things we would like to do in this life. Still, I have made a renewed resolution to confront my procrastination and to follow the leading of the Holy Spirit with more abandon.

Mildred, THANK YOU!

The Cloistered Tomato

Today, a hot July day, I was in the market buying fresh fruits and vegetables. Glancing at a sign, I was puzzled to read "Cloister Tomatoes."

Cloistered tomatoes? They must have grown up in a very holy environment.

On second reading, I realized the sign actually read "Cluster Tomatoes." I think this means I'm overdue for a retreat!

Keys - Peter's, Elizabeth's, Yours, and Mine

What do your keys open? Jesus gave to PETER the keys of the kingdom of heaven.

"And I tell you, you are Peter, and on this rock I will build my church, and the gates of Hades will not prevail against it. I will give you the keys of the kingdom of heaven, and whatever you bind on earth will be bound in heaven, and whatever you loose on earth will be loosed in heaven (Matthew 16, 18-19)

Currently I have the keys to my neighbor Elizabeth's house. She is in her late nineties and is temporarily living with nearby relatives.

Every day, I unlock the front door of her home and open the curtains of the living room and bedroom windows. Before dark, I go back, take in the mail, and draw the curtains.

I miss Elizabeth so much, but feel happy that I am doing something to help take care of her beloved home while she is away.

Elizabeth's keys are not mine. They are only entrusted to me for a specific time and for a specific purpose. They belong to Elizabeth.

What are the keys you and I are holding in our hearts? Is there a key to unlock and to heal old memories deeply buried?

We may ask the Lord to find that key and to unlock that which we seem unable to unlock. We may ask the Lord to heal us and to free us.

Born to the Purple

Every school child knows that purple is a blend of two colors. Red and blue.

Red. Red reminds me of blood, the shed blood of Jesus on the Cross. The Cross in my own life. My own death to self.

Blue. The "blues." Grief, sadness. Blue is also the color associated with the Blessed Mother, the Mother of Jesus.

Red and blue blend into purple. Royalty. Christ the King.

Hermitation

I don't live in a hermitage and I'm not hibernating.

Still, this is a time in my life when I seem to need extra silence and rest.

Ecumenism on the Go

Two beautiful days in October, 2002! These days were packed to the hilt emotionally and spiritually.

On Thursday, I was at my usually Prayer Group. In this group, which meets in the church, we pray the Rosary, pray for the Church and the world, and pray for one another.

Then, I drove north for the All Church Prayer Group which met at that time in a church library. Christians of many denominations are usually in attendance at this group.

Today, however, Helen, our leader, was alone. For various reasons, no one else attended. Helen and I prayed and then ventured forth on a mission. One of the people we had just prayed for was a thirteen year old boy at Children's Hospital, awaiting a heart transplant. We decided to go and pray for him in person.

This was quite an adventure as we drove round and round looking for parking places. The Lord provided! First, I found a place to park, then hopped in Helen's car until she found a place.

The young patient was in a class, but we were allowed to meet with him briefly. He was so frail and so brave. We are asking the Lord to heal his heart in whatever way was best for him.

The next day, Friday, I attended a memorial service for a teenager at a Jewish temple in a nearby town. I had no idea of how I would be able to find a parking place at the memorial. Just after parking on a neighborhood street, a police officer came by and said parking was not allowed there.

Out of the blue, the owner of the home emerged and offered me a place to park in her driveway. A parking angel! A tremendously moving tribute to this talented, beautiful young high school student.

After leaving this service, I drove to noon Mass in my town and then proceeded north to another prayer group. This is an interdenominational group which meets and prays for our young adult children in college and careers.

Two draining, yet very rewarding days. A privilege to be in the place of prayer, a place within the heart of God.

The "crammed" days also were a reminder to balance this activity with times of silence and solitude. Thank you, Lord, for this time of rest.

Oil Billionaires

You are an oil billionaire! I am an oil billionaire, too.

As baptized Christians, filled with the Holy Spirit, often symbolized by oil in Sacred Scripture, we may make this startling statement, with complete honesty.

We are so rich! We are "oil" billionaires.

Come Holy Spirit. Please show us how to share these riches of your mercy with others.

"I Just Want to Go Home!"

Our town has been busy the last few weeks resurfacing the neighborhood streets. There have been notices about which streets would be closed which days.

One day, last week, I was driving from downtown back home. As it became clear that all surrounding streets, as well as our own street, was blocked off, I was getting frightened.

How would I get home? With my current foot problem, how far could I walk?. A city worker motioned me to another route. I tried to go there, but it was closed.

Getting really anxious, I was aware that there was yet another way I had not tried. Then, I parked and walked home.

Home. We have such deep emotions about this word and all it represents.

This is the day before Thanksgiving 2002. Dusting my grandmother's sideboard, filled with photos of family and friends, I was seized with such a simultaneous sense of nostalgia and gratitude.

Gratitude. Thank you, Lord, for the gift of family and friends.

Nostalgia. It hurts not to be able to be with all of them.

Yet, there will be a time of going Home. Home to our Father. Home.

Power of Five

Five minutes. What can be accomplished in such a short time?

Instead of attempting super-heroic feats of whatever, I am trying to learn to break life and all its requirements into thinner segments.

Instead of feeling guilty for not praying an hour, I can take a "prayer break" and sit quietly in the Lord's presence for five minutes. Surely that is better than fretting because I can't drive to the monastery and be before the Blessed Sacrament for an hour.

Household chores. This morning I was able to break a few cleaning jobs into short segments. When the timer beeped, I would stop. Well, usually. Sometimes I did reset the timer.

Lord Jesus, you are Lord of time and eternity. Please help to me to flow in your time, your "kairos" and accomplish what you think is the most important.

The Captain Who Scrubbed the Decks

Advent, 2002. The Light of Christ is deeply penetrating into our lives.

Jesus is the Head of the Church and has promised that the gates of hell will not prevail against his Church, his Body on this earth. This is made clear in Matthew 16,18. These are the words of Jesus to Peter.

Jesus, is the "captain" of our salvation (Hebrews 2, 10, KJV). He is also the humble, suffering Servant.

Jesus kneels on the deck of his Church and lovingly, yet inexorably scrubs. His precious Blood flows over the Church.

When he comes again in glory, he will come for a pure, spotless Bride, a Church purified and refined. The purification happening now is necessary.

Lord Jesus, thank you for the work of cleansing you are accomplishing in our lives. Thank you for your humility and majesty. Have mercy upon us.

31

What Card Are You Holding Up to Your World?

In the fall of 1985, I studied New Testament Greek at Fuller Theological Seminary at the Menlo Park Extension Program. Class was Monday night from 7:00 - 10:00 p.m. The students were from all over the Bay Area. Some drove long distances to be in this class.

Our professor was a gentle Presbyterian pastor. He was very astute about advising us how to study. When we seemed overwhelmed, he would scale back the assignments for awhile.

During the week, when Christopher was in school, I diligently studied Greek. This was one of the most time-consuming and demanding courses I ever took.

One little study aid was to write vocabulary words on note cards. I would write the Greek on one side and the English on the other. Over the course of the week, I would try to memorize the new words.

Once, I was to meet a friend, Barbara, at a park and then we would maybe go somewhere for coffee. While waiting for Barbara, I took out my latest stack of cards. I walked around the park, holding up cards to see if I remembered what the word was.

One card was the Greek word for "fear." I was puzzled when a woman in the park gave me an alarmed look.

No wonder! I was holding up the Greek word, "phobos," which only I could see. The only word she could see written on the other side was "FEAR."

What sort of "card," or message is my life holding up to the world? The world can't see my side of the card.

Lord Jesus, you can see what is on my side of the card and what message is being projected to the world around me. Thank you for continuing to heal me and to fill me with you love. Let the message I hold up to others be one of life and hope.

The Truth Sayers
(December 14, 2002, St. John of the Cross)

Not very blessed, according to the world's standards, are those who speak the truth, for they shall be misunderstood, criticized, and may be thrown out of organization.

Their cheerleaders are not in the boardroom, but rather in the great cloud of witnesses (Hebrews 12, 1) in the ranks of the patriarchs, prophets, apostles, and saints.

"Wherefore seeing we also are compassed about with so great a cloud of witnesses, let us lay aside every weight, and the sin which doth so easily beset us, and let us run with patience the race that is set before us, Looking unto Jesus the author and finisher of our faith; who for the joy set before him endured the cross ... and is ... at the right hand of the throne of God (Hebrews 12, 1-2 KJV)."

Commandvitation

The Lord, through a series of circumstances, seems to be inviting/commanding me to "come apart and rest awhile." (Mark 6, 31).

Some time, quite some time ago, I perceived this as invitation. I was foolish enough to think I could delay answering this invitation. I wasn't doing anything terrible. In fact, I was doing lots of "good" things. Prayer groups, etc. They just weren't the things that God wanted me to be doing with the majority of my time any more.

A medical test, requiring a biopsy, has changed the "invitation" into a command. I had no choice but to be brave and spend more time alone in the Lord's presence.

What am so afraid of? I am afraid of facing myself.

True, I face myself and find freedom each time I celebrate the sacrament of reconciliation. Still, ...

Lord Jesus, guide me gently into this new pasture of rest and reflection. Thank you for the still waters. Thank you for your presence. Thank you.

Command Performance

No, this "performance" is not going to be on a stage. The Lord and the saints in glory will see, but others will not.

They are not the audience. As someone wisely said, "I live my life before an audience of ONE."

This new way of living is for the Lord. Somehow, my task is to continue to care for others, to reach out to others, and yet to care for myself.

There is no energy for people-pleasing. There is no anointing for self-promotion. Time in God's presence. The rest that precedes the restoration.

Put Down Your Pompons!

This strange command surfaced as I drove home from Mass. "Put down your pompons." Cheerleaders jump up and down and wave pompons, you know.

At one time, feeling I had no life, in a sense, I took up spiritual cheerleading. I would affirm and encourage and cheer others on.

There is nothing wrong with that, per se. My problem was that I had let it become a substitute for living out my own vocation within its strict and unusual confines.

I continue to be an encourager, but from another perspective, within another dynamic. The borders or confines of my life do allow me a rare freedom.

Lord Jesus, help me to live and move and breathe within the

spacious land of hope in which you have planted me. Help me to remember that fidelity to your call, to your invitation, is what you are seeking from me.

A Knife and a Rosary?

Several years ago, there were reports in our part of town of someone attacking early morning joggers. One of my neighbors was frightened when she thought someone was following her.

I don't jog, but I do walk a bit. Occasionally, as did one of my professors in the seminary, I carry a rosary as I walk. Once, to be doubly prepared, I wondered if I should also carry a knife in one pocket and a rosary in the other! No.

Rats, the Gregorian, and the Solemnity of Mary

January 1, 2003. The Solemnity of Mary.

This was definitely a mystics and mashed potatoes day.

Right before leaving for Mass, the humane trap in the garage seemed to have an inhabitant. Then the rat or whatever it isescaped! We've been trying to catch whatever it is and then release it in the arboretum on the Stanford campus.

The noon Gregorian Mass was beautiful! Seeing a friend, Caroline, at the Mass was a delightful surprise.

A gently glorious sunset. Hope for the new year.

Don't Cloud your Witness

I was struggling with a certain habit which I know displeases God. It is necessary, not only to exercise prudence, but also to pray for God's grace to do what I cannot do on my own.

As I prayed for help, I remembered the book of Hebrews

12, 1, where the author refers to the great "cloud of witnesses" which surrounds us as we continue our pilgrimage Home. It occurred to me that, as witnesses ourselves, we can be sources of clarifying or clouding the message of Christ to those around us.

Lord Jesus, help me to lay aside anything in my life which would "cloud" your ability to use me as a witness to You.

Mystics and Manicures

Once in a while I like to get a manicure. It's fun to have someone fuss over you and make your nails pretty.

Last week-end, after a conference, Terry and I were in the San Diego airport waiting to catch the return flight home. A lively group of high school girls were in the same waiting area for the flight before ours.

They were cheerleaders returning from a competition, I believe. They were having fun giving manicures to each other, laughing, and curling their eyelashes.

Jokingly, I held up my hands to the "manicurist" and asked, "Two tacos for a manicure?" There was a fast food taco place right there in the airport.

Sarah, the cheerleader, responded, "No, I want to do this out of the goodness of my heart." She proceeded to transform my nails to a dazzling, lovely coral color. She finished just in time before the boarding began for her flight.

Although I had thanked her profusely, I still wanted to express my thanks. Remembering the contents of my purse, I reached in and pulled out a simple little pink rosary.

Jumping up, I ran over to the waiting line and called "Sarah." She turned around, but missed seeing me. I was able to put the rosary in the hands of one of the mother chaperones to give her.

This was a very touching little incident. I had needed a little "lightening up" after the conference. A manicure from a cheerleader was just what the Holy Spirit ordered!

Feeding the Locusts

"And I will restore to you the years that the locust hath eaten ..." (Joel 2, 25, KJV). This verse has been a comfort to countless Christians over the years. It is especially comforting when "bad" things happen outside our volition.

Sometimes, though, I give in to the worry that, "What if I fed the locusts?"

What about the results that I have brought about by my own poor choices? Choices driven by anger, fear, etc.?

Comfort is found in Romans 8, 28 (NRSV). "We know that all things work together for good for those who love God, who are called according to his purpose."

Somehow, in the mystery of the divine economy, God will be glorified even in my wrong choices. The key is to keep turning to God, asking for forgiveness and for eventual restoration.

Pump Gas and Die!

After my mother moved from earth to heaven in the summer of 2001, I made a little note in my Morehouse Christian pocket diary to learn to pump gas and to write out my own funeral plans. Well, here it is almost Lent in 2003 and I still haven't completed these simple tasks.

Over the years, I have avoided the simple task of pumping gas. Either my husband has done it or I have patronized a station with Wednesday specials on the "Full Serve" side. One station had a "Ladies' Day" special until an attorney threatened to sue, calling it discrimination.

Then the station took down its sign, but offered discounts to anyone, as long as the minimum purchase was for eight or more gallons. The main reason I've avoided this is my lack of mechanical skill. I just get very nervous when I'm alone with machines. The fact that I'm typing this into a computer, or is it a word processor, is a miracle.

So grateful for Carol, Ginny, Molly, Jan, and other friends who encourage me to keep writing. Once, I was in the check-out lane at Trader Joe, when I saw Helen, one of my seminary professors, in the next lane. She called out, "Keep writing!" I really needed encouragement that day.

Back in college, I participated in a survey research class in political science. Each student was to drive out into the rural counties surrounding the university and interview farmers. That part was fun, Writing the results was fun.

What was not fun was feeding the card sorter with the punched results from the interviews. I was alone in a room in the Political Science building. Alone with a card sorter!

Decades later I still don't know what really happened. All of a sudden, the machine started sputtering out cards everywhere. Terrified, I ran downstairs to a secretary's office. "Help! I confess! I did it! I overfed the card sorter!"

Then the horror recurred! This time I was working one summer in a hospital in a Clinical Pastoral Education program. The ministry with the patients was wonderful. Meetings with my chaplain colleagues and our saintly supervisor, the Rev. Dr. Carlton Young, were inspiring, challenging and comforting.

Working with the computer was terrifying! I tried so hard to write down all the instructions. Going to the computer and trying to remain calm, I typed in what I thought was the list of patients I was to see that day.

All of a sudden. the computer went insane and chugged out the names of all the patients in the hospital! I couldn't stop it. Reams of paper were rolling out all over the floor. Again, I ran for the secretary's office. "I confess!" "Help!" She calmly followed me to the scene of the crime, stopped the machine, and helped me to know which patients to see.

Why me, O Lord? I try to get along with mechanical objects. This is just hard for me.

As far as the "die" part, maybe it's better if I just write out the funeral plans. I love liturgy and am definitely more confident in this area than in pumping gas.. I'd pretty much planned out Mother's memorial service before her departure. As I sat by her hospital bed for the last time, I said, "Mother I hope you like this. I'm trying to make it pretty for you." LaVelle, Mother's Methodist minister, was with us both at the hospital and at the church and was wonderful. I persuaded her to wear white vestments instead of those black Geneva gowns, or whatever they are called.

There have been multiple opportunities over the years to specify my funeral wishes. The Episcopal church where I had served as a field ed. seminarian had forms in the office. There was an opportunity in the chaplaincy program. A few years ago, a Catholic parish had an excellent Lenten program on "Death and Dying." Again, forms were passed out so we could specify our wishes for our funerals.

Why I am so hesitant? It's not because I don't think I'll die. Well, maybe if Jesus returns first, I won't.

What is the real reason? From my time of silence today in monastery, I have a clue.

It is a fear that I haven't done all God wanted me to do while on this earth. True, I have tried to walk through the doors the Holy Spirit has opened for me. There is a passion to have the liturgy reflect what I have tried to accomplish in this life.

At any rate, I'll rustle up a little something this Lent for the memorial. Maybe I'll even go to a station and learn to pump gas!

N.B. Since writing this reflection, I have learned to pump gas. Also, I have written out the plans for my send-off and have given the information to three trusted priests.

Outdated Prescriptions

What is not longer working in my life? Do I need to go to the Divine Physician and ask for a new direction and a new prescription?

Old formulas for prayer may need to be discarded in order for the Holy Spirit to breathe new freshness into my spirit. Just as I would not be wise to continue to take a long-expired prescription for my physical health, I would be very wise to check with the Holy Spirit and my spiritual director about the medicine I have been taking for my soul and spirit. Perhaps a new prescription is in order.

Are You a Broadcaster or a Forecaster?

A good broadcaster or a good reporter factually and faithfully states the news. The "news" may be mundane or terrifying. The reporter's role is to relay the news.

A forecaster, on the other hand, has studied the facts and then made a prediction. A weather forecaster may study the storms out in the ocean and then predict what the weather will be like in our area.

A faithful forecaster of God's promises is, in truth, a prophet. A true prophet of God speaks forth God's message before the fact.

Abraham, our father in the faith, was one the most fascinating forecasters of all time. The fourth chapter of Romans relates how the elderly Abraham stubbornly and radically chose to believe in God, to believe that God's outrageous, seemingly impossible promise of progeny, would actually happen! He was about a hundred years old and his wife was way beyond the years of childbearing.

St. Paul referred to Abraham as the father of us all (Romans 4,16). Abraham prevailed "… in the presence of God in whom he believed, who gives life to the dead and calls into existence the things that do not exist. Hoping against hope, he believed that he would become 'the father of many nations' ..." (Romans 4,17,18 NRSV). "No distrust made him waver concerning the promise of God, but he grew strong in his faith as he gave glory to God, being fully convinced that God was able to what he had promised (Romans 4, 20,21 NRSV)."

Today, I have to decide whether to be a broadcaster or a forecaster. Which will I choose?

If I decide to be a broadcaster, I simply state the facts, hopeless or exalted though they seem to be.

If, on the other hand, I choose to be a forecaster, I focus on the promise of GOD, impossible though it seems.

Trust in GOD is the decisive difference. Perhaps that is the difference between the two.

A broadcaster, or a reporter, is a realist. Trust is not needed simply to state the obvious.

A forecaster, however, acknowledges the truth of the broadcast, but focuses on GOD who is more powerful than any gloomy prediction of forecast.

Dear Lord, please strengthen me to continue to trust that no matter how long it takes, your promises will come to pass.

Department of Consecration

Under the palm tree! I was sitting outside under the palm tree on a warm April afternoon, taking a little break from putting all the furniture back after having had the carpets cleaned.

Glancing over a little brochure describing various Earth Day events, I noticed that one of the events was made possible by a grant from the Department of Consecration.

Department of Consecration? Blinking, I looked again at the brochure. The words were actually "Department of Conservation!"

Well, it's Lent, so I guess "consecration" is on my mind. Leviticus 21, 7b-8 NRSV refers to priests as sacred or "holy to their God, and you shall treat them as holy, since they offer the food of your God; they shall be holy to you, for I the Lord who sanctify you, am holy."

Holiness. Consecration. Sanctification.

Do these seem impossible ideals? We know our God is holy.

The ones around God's throne sing ceaselessly and prostrate themselves in the presence of God. "Holy, holy, holy, the Lord God the Almighty, who was and is and is to come (Revelation 4,8 NRSV)."

God commands us to be holy. "For I am the Lord your God; sanctify yourselves therefore, and be holy, for I am holy." (Leviticus 11, 44a NRSV).

We are not left alone in this department of consecration. The God who calls us to be holy is always in charge.

At the Annunciation, the Blessed Virgin Mary asked, not "why," but "how."

"How can this be …(Luke 1, 34, NRSV)?"

The answer was "The Holy Spirit …(Luke 1,35)."

The same Holy Spirit will accomplish God's purpose for our lives as we cooperate in loving and trusting obedience

"May the God of peace himself sanctify you entirely; and may your spirit and soul and body be kept sound and blameless at the coming of our Lord Jesus Christ. The one who calls you is faithful, and he will do this (1 Thessalonians 5,23-24 NRSV)."

Alleluia in advance!

AWAY!

John the Baptist looked at Jesus and proclaimed, "Here is the Lamb of God who takes away the sin of the world! (John 1, 29b NRSV)."

When we confess our sins, we are forgiven, but may have a lingering sense that our sins are still "out there" somewhere. This is not true.

Our sins are gone. Jesus, the Lamb of God, has taken them AWAY!

The sacrament of reconciliation is truly a sacrament in which we celebrate our freedom. We are free! Jesus has taken our sins away.

A Larger Circle

How do you treat people who behave in ways that are cruel? Don't try to destroy them. They're already spiritually, morally, and emotionally dead or they wouldn't treat others in such cruel ways.

Don't try to destroy them with your anger. They're already dead. Instead, pray to love them to Life.

So what if they don't want you or don't need you or exclude you? So what?

"He drew a circle that shut me out --
Heretic, rebel, a thing to flout.
    But Love and I had the wit to win:
We drew a circle that took him in."

(from Edwin Markham's poem "Outwitted")

Balloons Ready for the Release

National political conventions! Although there are always sharp differences of opinion on candidates and issues, there is still something that brings joy to all.

Balloons! On the ceilings, huge numbers of balloons are contained. They are held together waiting for the big moment to be released.

Sometimes when we are weary and discouraged, it helps to think of God's gifts this way. In spite of our feelings, God has not forsaken us. God has countless blessings all stored up waiting for just the right time to release them.

H-O-P-E!

Under the palm tree. Late this afternoon, I was sitting under the palm tree, feeling extremely discouraged. The Lord seemed to insert the word "hope" into my weary heart.

H could stand for Honor God. O for Optimism. P for Pray. E for Expect! H-O-P-E.

HOPE! My mood lifted with the gentle breeze waving under the palm tree.

The Swimming Rosary

I was trying to decide what to do with my mind while I was lap swimming. Staring at other swimmers and the lifeguards gets boring after a while.

So, I decided to pray the rosary. Not holding an actual rosary, but simply silently praying the rosary. I was concerned about the daughter of a friend. So, as I prayed the Joyful Mysteries, I prayed for this young girl.

For the first Joyful Mystery, the Annunciation, I prayed for the time the young girl had still been in her mother's womb. There is so much research and medical evidence of the importance of our time in the womb.

What the mother thinks and speaks, as well as what the mother eats, affects the unborn child. The Lord, who transcends what we call time, is able go back and to heal the memories from the time in the womb.

I progressed on, praying as I swam. It is not something I do every single time I swim, but was a new adventure in prayer.

From Mass to The Surfer Babe in One Not so Easy Ecumenical Week

Well, at least God knows I did my best and I believe Fr. Frank Norris (my thesis director in the seminary and my sponsor when I was received into the Roman Catholic Church) from his heavenly perch approves. This was a week with more than I bargained for.

It began last Saturday night with the reception for friends and family for a young couple (the groom had been raised Catholic) who had had a Protestant minister officiate at their wedding in another place. The photos were lovely and I am very happy for them. Also sad that there was no nuptial Mass.

After Mass on Wednesday (Monday and Tuesday, at that time, were my "poustinia" days of solitude), I felt strongly led to drive to a friend's house in a nearby town. "Hop in," I said, "I'm kidnapping you. We are going to drive to your church to pray for your ministry and for the Vacation Bible School."

When we arrived at the church, the pastor prayed with us and for us. We walked all around the church laying hands on every pew and praying, praying, praying for all the people who would be there for the adults-included Vacation Bible School.

Well, wouldn't you know it, that church had problems with

church politics. Jealousies. Blah, blah, the usual. So what else is new?

This week, not that it seemed to do much good, I prayed for a leader very very high up in academic circles who was to give a lecture on faith in the work place. My hopes were dashed as the speaker seemed more intent on being politically correct. Dear Lord, I prayed, please don't let the people I invited be here. This speaker isn't talking about Jesus at all.

Tamales! Terry consoled me on the way home by stopping at our favorite Mexican restaurant and getting me a tamale. This did help calm me down!

Then I found out that one person I invited did come, but she was a strong Catholic. She was also mad about the talk, but not mad at me for inviting her.

Friday. The Queenship of Mary. God knows we need Mary. Blessed Mother, help us. Your Son is Head of the Church. He is a lot more patient than I am with church politics.

After a two hour ecumenical prayer group and lunch, I headed for a monastery for a time of silence. Then I stopped at the library of the seminary to check on something.

On the way home, I stopped at a favorite stationers. In addition to all the lovely stationery, the store has started to carry hand lotion, etc. One brand was called Surfer Babe! Tried a little sample. Now I smell like a coconut.

The market and home. E-mail news. A clergy friend has cancer surgery scheduled. Another clergy friend, a Protestant, made the mistake of becoming more popular than the senior pastor. She was removed.

Balance, balance, and more balance. Fortunately this was not a typical week.

Dear Lord, I need help in being able to care and console without becoming exhausted and discouraged. Thank you for tamales and that coconut surfer lotion!

Expectations

To expect to be validated in this world is to have invalid expectations!

As long as I am following the Lord as well as I can, that's all that matters.

Arena of Service

"Arena". That's what I thought it said.

Then I read it again. The announcement for a particular ministry actually read "area" of service.

Ministry, alas, does sometimes become an arena. Those who are there to minister, sometimes become competitors.

They compete with one another in subtle, or not so subtle, ways to promote themselves. No one is exempt from this.

We all want to be appreciated. We all want to be noticed.

We are all growing in maturity if we are satisfied with the smile of God. We can serve in the area without competing in the arena.

Give UP!

Sometimes I just feel like giving up. Everyone feels this way at one time or another.

Winston Churchill said NEVER to give in! In his 1941 speech at Harrow School, he said, "Never give in – never, never, never, never, in nothing great or small, large or petty, never give in except to convictions of honour and good sense. Never yield to force; never yield to the apparently overwhelming might of the enemy."

UP! Maybe the solution is to give the situation UP to God.

Good Grief or Gray Grief

Black! Black grief is real and rends the heart. Mourning is necessary.

Gray! Gray grief is the result of an incompletely mourned loss.

This kind of loss is so incorporated into the essence of the person that all of life is viewed through a blurry gray lens.

Physical illness is one thing, but "... a wounded spirit who can bear (Proverbs 18.14 KJV)?"

King David, the psalmist was well acquainted with mourning. He eventually was able to rejoice. "Thou hast turned for me my mourning into dancing ... (Psalm 30, 11 KJV)."

Lord Jesus, please heal any residual grief within me. Let me again sing "Alleluia!"

Who Is Your Image Consultant?

GOD!

You are created in the image of God. I am created in the image of God.

God is our image consultant.

It is how GOD sees us that matters.

The Struggling Butterfly

Needing a bit of warmth during winter, we drove one Saturday to

San Francisco to the Conservatory of Flowers in the Golden Gate Park.

Bliss! It was warm and fragrant inside. Bright tropical flowers, exquisite water lilies, singing fountains, and chattering children running all over.

In one of the rooms, there was an exhibit of butterflies in the process of emerging from their protective chrysalises. One particular butterfly was struggling to emerge. It was only part of the way out. It would struggle and then rest. The docent said that this had been going on all day.

According to the docent, a seven year old boy had been in the conservatory earlier in the day and was watching the struggling butterfly. He quietly commented, "Some births take longer than others. I know. Mine did."

After a while, we went back to the room with the fountain and water lilies. Every so often, Terry would go back and check on the progress of the butterfly.

Finally, it was getting close to closing time. I stood one last time looking at the butterfly, hoping and praying it would be able to get out. I still don't know if it did.

How God must yearn over us to emerge into the fullness of life. How we struggle and wonder if we will make it.

"Some births take longer than others."

Feeding or Starving

Am I holding a grudge? Am I holding it and feeding it as a mother feeds her beloved child?

Or I am starving the grudge by releasing it to God and refusing to speak of it?

What we feed will keep growing. What we starve will eventually fade away. This does not mean we forget. It means that we are living, finally, in another realm.

Prayer Chickens

The old saying about chickens coming home to roost can have a positive meaning. When we pray and pray and nothing seems to change, we still pray and wait and trust.

The prayer chicks will one day be on the horizon and come home to roost. We will rejoice then. Why don't we rejoice right now before we see the answer?

Growing into Your Vocation

Sometimes when I see an old dress I would really like to be able to wear again, it's a good motivation to hang it up somewhere so I see it everyday. Then I can decide to eat less and exercise more so I can fit into it again.

It's different with our spiritual lives. Instead of shrinking a bit, we want to expand a lot! Grow!

We want to trust God that, little by little, we are growing into the work he has for us to do. True, we are doing something now, but it is not all that God has for us. God always has more.

Cheerio!

The first time I ever preached in an Episcopal church on a Sunday morning, a friend, an ordained minister in the Episcopal Church, came to be supportive. She and her family sat in the very last pew.

When I preached, I was very aware of people as individuals. It was as if I was not preaching to a "congregation," but to each person, including myself, on a very individual basis.

I was puzzled when I saw my friend dipping down and coming back up again. What in the world was she doing?

I found out later that one of her little boys was dropping little round cereals onto the floor and she was retrieving them, The old game of "See Mummy Fetch!"

The Bridge

Bridges. Do you remember the French folk song, "Sur Le Pont d'Avignon?"

In my study, I have framed prints of bridges. There is one of the bridge near Kings' College in Cambridge.

There is another of the bridge at Monet's estate, Giverney. This is the one with the water lilies.

Bridges fascinate me.

The dictionary says the word "bridge" means a structure used to carry a road over an obstacle or a depression. The word "pontifex," from which we get the word "Pope" literally means a bridge- maker.

Once, when I was in my study, working at the computer, the phone rang. It was a very difficult time in my life. I am very glad I took the call. It was a woman I didn't really know that well, from a Catholic prayer group, with a message for me.

I believe it was a message from God, although the person calling me probably did not know that. She simply called to tell me something.

"You are a bridge," she told me. "What happens to bridges? They get walked on." That was it!

I thanked her, because it was truly a message of confirmation and comfort. Yes, bridges get walked on, but that is not all.

God uses bridges to get people from one place to another. The bridge does not understand this, but God understands.

Did Jesus Throw Out the Forty Days?

Last Sunday, one of the hymns began, "Lord, who throughout these forty days .... " Terry, who had not quite found the page, inquired, "He threw out the forty days?!"

Jesus threw out all our sins when he died on the Cross. He threw them out by taking them into himself.

WE were crucified with Jesus on the Cross. (Galatians 2, 19-20) When Jesus died on the Cross, we died.

We are now FREE for the risen Lord Jesus Christ to live in us, through the power of the Holy Spirit. St. Paul did his best to teach us about this, but it still takes us a lifetime to begin to grasp the wonder of it all.

The Red Carpet

Do you watch the Academy Awards on television? If you do. you notice the red carpet. The stars walk in on the red carpet.

At Prayer Group yesterday, I was looking at the red carpet in the church. It is in the aisles and leads to the altar.

Jesus, the Star, is there.

Nehemiah Ate Tin?

What did Nehemiah, the king's cup bearer, eat?

Tin? Ten?

If you just hear the words "Nehemiah 8, 10, " spoken aloud, you might wonder.

In the book of Nehemiah, Ezra, the priest and scribe, was talking about strength! He told the people not to be sad, because rejoicing in the Lord was their strength! (Nehemiah 8, 10) The walls of Jerusalem had been rebuilt.

We too will rejoice when the Lord has completed his work of rebuilding and restoration in our lives. Meanwhile, the joy of the Lord is our strength!

Stretching

Recently, I bought a new pair of shoes. The left one fits fine, but the right one is a little tight. I took it back to the store to be stretched.

Stretched. We are constantly being stretched in this life.

Stretched to endure. Stretched to have hope. Stretched to do what God wants us to do.

I take comfort from the words of St. Paul to the Philippians. Paul referred to forgetting the past and stretching forward to what lies ahead, the prize of the high calling of God in Jesus Christ.

" … this one thing I do, forgetting those things that are behind, and reaching forth unto those things that are before, I press for the mark, for the prize of the high calling of God in Christ Jesus (Philippians 3, 13, 14 KJV)."

The Jazz Frogs

Some years ago, we had a compact disc of summer nature sounds, in this case, the sounds of frogs. There was a sense of a warm, lazy, summer afternoon.

Terry decided to make a cassette copy of this frog music. Not noticing that the tape was in the machine, I turned on the local jazz station on the radio.

Later, when we played the tape, there was a surprise! The frogs were droning on and on, and then suddenly there was a loud burst of jazz!

It was as if the frogs woke up from their nap, grabbed their instruments, and decided to become a little dance band. Maybe it's time to wake up and dance!

Grace Before Time

Recently I was studying 2 Timothy 1, 8, 9. Amazing, isn't it, to ponder God's ways! God's grace was given to us even before the beginning of what we call time.

Paul wrote, "Do not be ashamed, then, of the testimony about our Lord or of me his prisoner, but join with me in suffering for the gospel, relying on the power of God, who saved us and called us with a holy calling, not according to our works but according to his own purpose and grace. This grace was given to us in Christ Jesus before the ages began ...(2 Timothy 1, 8, 9a NRSV)."

The grace we know we need has already been given to us. It was given before the beginning of time, even before the world began.

Prayer Makeover

Personal makeovers, involving new clothes and new haircuts, are fun and refreshing. House makeovers positively inspire us to clean house and rearrange a bit.

The kind of makeover I really need is a prayer makeover. Over the years, many ways of praying, valid though they are, are becoming old.

God is still the same, but I seek fresher ways of communicating. More silence. More trust. Less trying to be a fixer. More seeking to be an adorer.

An Honesty Day

Today, I felt anger that I did not know how to deal with. I was home alone and started to yell out to God about a troubling situation.

Freedom! Instead of trying to mask or ignore my feelings, I experienced the wonderful freedom of pouring my heart out to God and asking God to take over both the situation and my emotions.

Zipped, Not Zapped

Waiting. Waiting. Waiting.

Zipped! We are not being zapped or destroyed, although it may appear that way.

Just as a precious garment may be zipped into a protective carrier, God may zip our dreams and visions and goals for a time. It won't be forever.

Zipped in for future release. Zipped in for fulfillment beyond our wildest imaginings or expectations!

Kneeling to See Better

On the top shelf of a small, low, bookcase in our home, there is a crucifix, blessed by one of my seminary classmates and given to me by my beloved Ukrainian godmother, Ann.

Standing, I am looking down on the Crucified.

Kneeling, I am closer and see Jesus better.

Maybe I cannot kneel physically, but I am honoring the Lord with my entire being and the Lord understands.

Hold Your Horses

How often, as children, were we impatient? An adult would try to help us to wait by telling us to "hold our horses."

Recently, while reading Gabrielle Bossis' tender book, <u>He and I</u>, I noticed a reference to horses. The reference was to the control of our thoughts.

Just as the driver of a carriage would tighten the reins to prevent the horse from bolting, we are to hold our thoughts in check for the sake of the Lord.

The Man Who Listened

He worked at the hospital as a custodian. Then, someone at the hospital discovered his special gift.

He listened. He REALLY listened!

He listened so well that a new vocation opened up for him. For at least part of his day, he listened.

Hospital employees came to him to pour out their problems. He listened. He did not counsel. He just listened, really listened, most likely with compassion and prayer.

A Frog, A Cricket, and Why

When we lived in Richardson, Texas, near Texas Instruments, we were in an apartment complex with a leafy courtyard. Very pleasant, except for the time I accidentally stepped on a toad! I still remember the awful squishy sound and the rubbery feel. The toad was pretty much all right, but I was unnerved.

Not as unnerved, however, as the time we were driving back from Dallas on North Central Expressway. We kept hearing some kind of chirping sound in the car. Chirp! chirp! chirp! A friendly, but puzzling chirp.

We arrived home and were walking between the parking lot and our apartment when I realized the chirping sound came from a cricket and the cricket was in my dress. I started screaming, not loud screaming, but muffled, sort of, and started to rip off my dress. Terry managed to get me inside the apartment and we freed the cricket.

Later, Terry said how glad he was that the cricket was not discovered as we drove down the expressway. It might have been hard for him to explain to the judge why his wife started to scream, ripped off her dress, and jumped out of a moving car!

Well, at this apartment complex, there was a wonderful man named Why. That really was his name!

Why was in charge of caring for the buildings and grounds. I asked him about his unusual name. He said that his parents already had quite a large family and that he was not expected. When he was born, all his mother could say was, "WHY?"

And so, Why became his name. I hope his mother later realized what a wonderful man her son became. Why was always very cheerful and positive.

He brought a beautiful sense of peace wherever he went. Why? Because. Because the world needed him.

Red Cannas at the Convent

Early in the morning, I decided to go north to Mass at a convent and then go south to a prayer group and then to go east to meet with yet another prayer group.

Traffic, traffic, traffic on the way to Mass. Construction all over the grounds of the convent. Parking problems. Finally, I blew in the door only to find out that Mass had been scheduled for another time at another place.

Already very frazzled, I managed to drive through all the

construction to leave. As I rounded the dark red brick building, I saw red cannas!

Blazing bright red cannas. Bold and brilliant cannas. There had been cannas, scarlet red cannas in my grandmother's garden in Texas. They are not my favorite of flowers, but I love to see them because they remind me of Nana and her house.

Suddenly, my day was restructured. I went to neither prayer group.

I had become over-extended in the matter of prayer groups, anyway. This was a day for God to come to me in other ways.

Red cannas at the convent.

Sow, Water, and Wait

The farmer sows the seeds and waters the seedlings. No wringing of hands and wondering and agonizing.

So with our prayers. We sow the seeds of our prayers into the lives of others. We water the little seedlings, even though we may not see them. We water them with our continued trust that God is working.

God is there. God is behind the scenes. God is working.

God's harvest will arrive in God's time.

Glory to God!

Saving Face or Seeking THE Face?

No one wants to look ridiculous. We have various ways of defending ourselves, especially if we think we are being criticized.

I want to learn to seek God's face, instead of being so motivated with saving face and seeking human approval.

The psalmist David prayed about beholding God's face (Psalm 17, 15). David endeavored to keep the Lord always before him (Psalm 16, 8) and to seek God's face (Psalm 27, 8).

St. Paul wrote that in our present lives we see only indistinctly or in a dim way, but that one day we will see distinctly, face to face (1 Corinthians 13, 12).

Until then, I want to seek God's face and to serve God's people, rather than being fixated on saving face.

In our society, so much energy is devoted to looking good, to the polishing of one's ego! Apologize? Forget it. Look good and forge ahead. Despise those who get in your way. Mow them down with your sarcastic, impatient words of criticism.

The mind-set described above is one increasingly encountered not only in the big world out there, but, alas, also encountered in those who profess to know God. Tragic.

Instead of trying to save face, we desperately need to seek GOD'S face. David the psalmist prayed that God's face would not be hidden from him (Psalm 27, 8).

David also prayed that God's face would shine upon him (Psalm 31, 16). As the apostle Paul noted, we now see dimly, but one day we will see face to face (1 Corinthians 13, 12).

The Lone Ranger Goes Scuba Diving

I just about jumped out of my skin when I walked into church as a weekday Mass was beginning. What in the world!?

The priest at the altar had some sort of mask on! He looked like a combination of the Lone Ranger and a scuba diver.

This wonderful, older priest had been struggling some time with his vision. With gentle determination, he presided at Mass, often using a large magnifying glass. We pray for him and thank God for the radiant witness of this holy, dedicated priest.

Write and Shine!

Since I am not currently serving in the more visible, active ways of ministry in which I served in the past, I've been a bit restless. Remembering the old injunction to rise and shine, I had some new insights.

Right now, my assignment is to write and shine! Ministry is always at God's call. Whatever my assignment is right now is what is best.

In the Potter's Hands

The Lord referred to Israel as clay in the hands of the potter, according to the prophet Jeremiah (Jeremiah 18. 5,6) When Jeremiah visited the house of the potter, he observed the potter refashioning spoiled clay into another vessel (Jeremiah 18,4).

Sometimes we may feel like a broken clay vessel. Life has taken us and smashed us into pieces.

The same God who raised Jesus from the dead (Romans 8, 11) can surely take the pieces of our lives and refashion them into a beautiful vessel. We are in the hands of a wise and loving Potter.

Into the Light

One October evening, I felt strongly led to attend a particular healing service in a Catholic church. The service began at 7:30 p.m. in the peaceful, candlelit church. The music and the prayers were beautiful. Later in the service, there would be an opportunity for individual prayer and then the prayer circle.

My heart had been heavy with the memory of a devastating experience some time before. At the prayer service, sitting alone in the church, I was given a new way to view this past event which was still affecting my life.

What happened in the service was not a "vision," but rather an interior understanding. I "saw" the room where this event occurred, the table, chairs, and the various people. At the time, I had felt abandoned.

Later, I would recall St. Paul' statement, "... no one came to my support, but all deserted me. May it not be counted against them! But the Lord stood by me and gave me strength ..." (2 Timothy 4, 16,17 NRSV).

In this prayer experience, I saw that the Lord was indeed there, seated at the head of the conference table. At the actual event, no one was in that chair. I was aware that it was JESUS, but all I saw were the tears falling from his eyes and down his face.

After some time, the Lord stood, walked to where I was sitting, took my hand and led me out of the room. We walked out of the room into an intensely bright, white light.

As I walked out the door into this light, I turned back to the room. The door had been left open, but the people in the room remained. The room was no longer an ordinary room, but a prison. I saw the bars. I turned back to the light and kept walking.

One last time I turned back to the room. It was no longer there. All was total darkness. This time I kept walking onto the light and prayed not to look back.

Years have passed since this experience. It is very healing to remember that the Lord, in his mercy, had removed me from a toxic situation and had placed me, instead, in another place where I could live and serve him with joy.

Water into Bread

Jesus turned water into wine! This is his first recorded miracle (John 2, 1-11). After this sign, his disciples believed in him. So, how can water be turned into bread?

Beautiful Graciela stopped by our house with a huge loaf of bread, designer bread, artisan bread. She had been going about the neighborhood giving out these loaves of bread. What in the world?!

Some time before, Graciela had been going to Watsonville to offer bottled water to those who labored in the fields, harvesting strawberries and all the other lovely produce we enjoy every day in California.

Then, one of the workers moved and took a job delivering bread to various stores. One day, he noticed Graciela and was so excited to see "the lady who brought us water!" He wanted to express his thanks by giving her bread, lots of bread.

Graciela is assured a reward for her kindness. Jesus said that giving a cup of water to one who bears the name of Christ will be rewarded (Mark 9, 41). Jesus turned the water Graciela gave in his Name into bread for many.

Bliss Blooms!

Surprise! A surprise was in store even though I had given up hope for this poor rose.

Years ago, we planted a "Sheer Bliss" rose under a palm tree. Not a wise choice, since the palm tree grew and grew and the rose was covered with shade.

Even so, the valiant rose persisted. It shot up high, pushing up through the fronds of the palm tree, and produced a bud! This lonely bud blossomed into a beautifully delicate and fragrant rose. It is a very pale pink and creamy color.

We kept procrastinating about trying to move the rose. There is so little sun in the back yard. The trees which were so little when we moved in are now towering over us. These are the sequoia redwoods, planted by previous owners. These trees are heritage trees, which are strictly protected by the city. We are not allowed to remove them.

Still, there was a bit of sun by the fence, so the rose was finally moved. It was seemingly very sad. Its leaves fell off and it just seemed like a pathetic bit of sticks.

Late in the summer, I broke my foot and was confined inside for a long time. By the time, I could get outside and see the fence, there was a big surprise. The "Sheer Bliss" had come back to life with a vengeance.

It shot up, grew new leaves, basked in the strength of the sun, enjoyed being watered, and produced buds and more buds. Beautiful "Sheer Bliss" roses!

When the first rose in the new location blossomed, I had been praying for some bit of encouragement. Terry said to look outside.

"Bliss" had finally been allowed to bloom!

Sometimes we are able to bloom where we are planted. Other times, we cannot bloom until we are transplanted.

The transplant may not be a geographical move. It may be a move within our souls to a new place of sunshine and hope.

God's Debutantes

White dresses! Flowers. Society. Introductions. Newspaper coverage.

God's redeemed will be presented to the King of the Universe and to all the company of heaven. They will stand before the throne of God and before Jesus, the Lamb of God, wearing white and holding palm branches. (Revelation 5, 9). What greater "society" could that be?

Love in a Package of Frozen Spinach

It was a typical church potluck dinner. People brought various dishes to share.

It was even called a Holy Spirit potluck, the idea being that the Holy Spirit would guide everyone about what to bring.

Well, the Holy Spirit decided to have a little fun with us that evening. One person brought some truly scary looking leftovers. At the table, they were politely passed from person to person. I don't know if anyone was brave enough to eat some or not.

What I do remember was the frozen spinach. After the dinner, someone came up to me and offered me a package of frozen spinach. It looked like it had been frozen and refrozen several times. She asked if I would like it.

I was stammering and trying to decide what to say. Impatiently, she glared at me and said, "Well, if you don't want it, just say so." I took the spinach, smiled, and said, "Thank you very much."

She offered what she had. It just took me awhile to respond, with gratitude, to the giver. Her intention was to share what she had. This is all that any of us can offer.

Mary at the Media Table

At a conference many years ago, I stopped at the media table to glance over the many different recordings.

As I glanced at the young woman at the table, I suddenly thought, "She looks life Mary!" I mean, THE Mary, the mother of Jesus.

The thought came to me so suddenly. This was long before I became a Catholic and I did not know about Marian devotion at all. There was something about the wise expression in the eyes of this gentle, beautiful young woman that caught my attention.

It does not matter whether or not this woman really did look like Mary. What I carried from the experience is that it is important to remember that Mary was a real person!

She experienced joy and sorrow, so much sorrow, in her life. And yet, she was the mother of Jesus. She was chosen from among all women for the honor of bearing and nurturing the Son of God.

Gospel Sparks

When I was in St. James, a church in Bosnia, in the late 1980's, something very unusual happened during Mass. At the time, I felt uncertain about sharing my experience.

At the reading of the Gospel, I would see "sparks." It looked as if many people over the crowded church were taking flash pictures, but they weren't!

Later, I was relieved to find out I was not the only one to see the sparks. For whatever reason, the Holy Spirit had decided to have a little fireworks show.

The Gospel always gives light. We may not always seen sparks, but the light is always there.

Comets and Candles

Comets are exciting! They burst on the scene in a blaze of glory.

Candles are quiet. They shed their gentle light and may flicker. They are usually unassuming and doubt themselves and their contributions. They wonder if they count. They have the promise of Isaiah 42, 3 that their light, even if it is dim and flickering, will not be quenched.

Brass Plates and the Lamb's Book

Last week, I stopped by a church for a few moments of solitude. As I left, I noticed a brass plate on the back wall. On it were engraved the names of people who had been especially singled out to be honored.

On another occasion, while visiting a school, I noticed brass plaques, engraved with the names of those who had contributed money to the school.

These honorable mentions are fine. It's good to notice, to affirm, and to recognize the contributions of time and other resources.

There is a book, however, that is of greater interest to me than the plaques. This is the Lamb's Book of Life, which is referred to in St. Paul's Letter to the Philippians (Philippians 4,3) and in the Revelation to St. John (Revelation 13, 8).

Whether or not our names are ever written in the brass plates of this world does not matter so much. Knowing our names are in the book of Jesus, the Lamb of God, is what matters. This is what brings us joy and peace.

The Corner Table

It was a cold, gray day in early winter and I was meeting a dear friend for coffee. I had been ill for a long time and was just getting out again.

Having arrived at the little bakery/cafe, I spotted two people just leaving the corner table by the window. Just as I was about to go and sit there, an older man from a nearby table, coffee cup in hand, leaped to his feet and rushed past me to claim the table.

"Looks like we both had the same idea," I said to him. All he said was, "Oh, yes, this one is so much better."

Shock vs. Holy

When the shock factor in our diseased society seems to be maxed out, we pray that the holiness factor be activated as we cry out to God for mercy and forgiveness.

God is holy and calls us to be holy, to be salt and light in this desperately sick society. Lord Jesus Christ, Son of God, have mercy on us.

Reaching Out

A friend had been going through a difficult time. Having just received a lovely book on a subject I knew was of deep interest to her, I wrote her a note and dropped the book off at her house.

Bad idea! She later called, not to thank me, but to complain about how she did not like the book and how the priest who had written the book could have done a better job. She went on and on and on.

I suggested, as calmly as possible, that she write a book and cover the subject in the way she thought best. She tossed that idea aside.

You know, God, sometimes I just get tired of reaching out to others. Do I go into a cave and become a hermit? Help me to remember to do what you call me to do and to leave the results with you.

The Bride's Room

This is the room in some churches where the bride puts the final touches on her gown, her veil, her jewelry, etc. She has attendants lovingly assisting her on this day of days.

When at last I go to meet my heavenly Bridegroom, I'm sure there will be some kind of bride's room. Others will help me with their prayers on this day off days, my birthday in heaven.

Enemy at the Gate!

Look! There's an "enemy" right here on our own gate.

I was sitting by the window early one morning, having my coffee. Francis, our now frail and elderly marmalade cat, was sitting peacefully beside me.

All of sudden, there was a noise outside. Another cat was sitting on OUR gate and brazenly staring at us. Francis jumped up and glared at the other cat.

On another occasion, a small, but determined dog was attempting to ram into the cat door in this gate. Francis looked really alarmed at that! Although he's getting on in years, Francis still zealously guards his property.

Are You Fighting with a Mirror?

Look in the mirror. Do see you see yourself as you really are?

At a nearby office building, a bird managed to fly upstairs and to "fight" with a security system mirror. The poor bird would peck away and peck away, but the bird in the mirror would not go away. Finally, in frustration, the little bird would fly back outside and return the next day for the same exercise in futility.

Are we fighting with ourselves? We do not see ourselves as others see us. We need a realistic, yet merciful, approach to the person in the mirror.

Integrated Circuitry of the Soul

Living in Silicon Valley, we hear all the time about circuits, transformers, etc. Our souls have circuits, too. Sometimes, it seems that our thoughts go round and round in the same dreary patterns.

St. Paul wrote about the re-wiring of our circuits, although he did not use those terms. He counseled not conformity to this world, but rather transformation achieved by the renewal of the mind so that the wonderful plan of God could be discerned (Romans 12, 2).

Snipping the Lavender

Late this morning, I drove by a particular white house with a white picket fence. Years ago, lavender bloomed profusely around the fence.

One day, I stopped to admire the lavender up close. Surprised and touched, I noticed a pair of scissors tied to the lavender, with a note to help oneself! How kind to share the lavender with those who appreciate this fragrant herb,

There is always something already in our possession that we have to share. What we consider of little value or interest may be just the thing that will touch the heart of another passerby.

A New Mansion

Today is April 4, 2005, two days after the death of our beloved Pope John Paul II. He has moved! He is now living in the house of his Father.

One of the television reporters noted that the Pope's last words on this earth were, "I am happy. You should be happy too."

When Nana, my maternal grandmother, died in 1981, I remember going to her house in Texas with my sister and my mother. We thought it would be devastating to walk into her house, knowing she would not be there.

We were touched and surprised to find Nana's dear friend, Helen, there waiting for us. She had prepared a lovely lunch for us. I started to cry and she said, "Don't grieve for Tommy." For some reason, Nana's close friends called her "Tommy" although here real name was Lydia.

Mother spoke some simple, yet profound words, which sustain me at this time when so many of us are grieving for our earthly shepherd. Mother simply said, "She (Nana) doesn't live here anymore."

Obviously! Yet these words were just what I needed to hear. Nana did not need to live in her house in Texas. She no longer needed to live in her earthly body.

As we honor this extraordinary Pope, we rejoice that he no longer lives in his frail, 84 year old, body. He is free! No more Parkinson's Disease or any other disease. He has moved to a new dwelling place, promised by Jesus.

Jesus, you remember, promised us that he himself would prepare a place just for us! "Do not let your hearts be troubled. Believe in God, believe also in me. In my Father's house there are many dwelling places. If it were not so, would I have told you that I go to prepare a place for you? I will come again and will take you to myself, so that where I am, there you may be also" (John 14, 1-3 NRSV).

Lines and Places

"Thy lines are fallen unto me in pleasant places …." This verse (Psalm 16. 6a) from the Kings James Version, popped into mind this morning. I had been feeling restless and frustrated with various limitations in my life.

Reading the verse and pondering it anew has helped me. The translation from the New Revised Standard Version shed new light, also." The boundary lines have fallen for me in pleasant places."

Lines and boundaries.

Yes! This place is pleasant. These boundary lines are pleasant. I will enjoy to the full this time and this place in my life.

Pilgrims of the Feet and Pilgrims of the Heart

This week in Rome has been like no other. So many pilgrims from all over the world have come to express their love for Pope John Paul II.

The Requiem Mass is tomorrow, April 8, 2005. The pilgrims patiently wait incredible hours in the lines that wind around and around the streets of Rome to St. Peter's Basilica to view the body, the earthly temple, of the Pope. One thinks of the words of the apostle Peter, who reminded us that we are indeed pilgrims and exiles here on earth. (1 Peter 2, 11).

For those who cannot be physically present in Rome, there is still the pilgrimage of the heart to make, We can pray for the spiritual and temporal needs of the pilgrims who are there in Rome as well as for ourselves as we keep vigil this week.

We weep, yet rejoice that this beloved servant of God is safely Home. We pray for all pilgrims, for our continued guidance and strength as we enter the final stretch of our own race, our own journey, our own pilgrimage.

The Veiled Lady

In times past, women in the Catholic Church and sometimes even in some Episcopal churches would always wear a mantilla, sometimes short, sometimes long, sometimes white, sometimes black, to every service at church. I recall photos of lovely Jacqueline Kennedy coming out of a Catholic church with her mantilla.

Once, after I became a Catholic, I was alone in church after an early Monday morning Mass. After some period of time, a sweet lady in a black mantilla walked up to me and asked if she could pray for me.

I was so touched by her concern. It doesn't matter if one wears a black mantilla or more contemporary attire. What matters is what is in the heart. What matters is that we express the love of God to others.

On Second Thought

"Good grief," I thought most uncharitably, to myself. He approaches the altar in a most tentative way. He slouches into the presider's chair. Doesn't he realize he is a PRIEST? Where is the dignity of his holy office? Why doesn't he at least comb his hair?

A little later in the liturgy, I quickly asked God's forgiveness for making such a hasty judgment of his appearance and his demeanor. God didn't ask to me judge, anyway. That's God's province.

The priest offered a truly beautiful homily. There was humor. There was humility. There was also evidence of a deep level of scholarship that had gone into that homily.

We just can't tell about other people. They are continually surprising us. Are we continually surprising others?

$43.10

Not once, but twice. Twice in one morning.

First, I went to Macy's to purchase cosmetics. A rare occurrence, since I try to buy only during the bonus times. The bill was $43.10, much more than I usually would dream of spending. The woman at the counter had been enthusiastic and even did a mini-make-up demonstration.

Next errand. This one I was dreading. I had bought a shirt that had distressingly disintegrated and was fraying. It was from one of the major mail order companies. The representative with whom I had spoken earlier, on the 800 customer service phone line, had told me simply to return it to the local store for either a refund or an exchange, She had been very polite and professional.

Not so at the nearby store. Suffice it to say that I was grudgingly granted a refund on my credit card. I said "thank you" and was happy to leave.

Surprise! It had to be one of God's loving surprises. When I checked the amount of the receipt, it was $43.10!

Fine-Tuning

The channel is set, the program is there, but the reception is fuzzy. I can hear, but not very well. I can see, but not very well.

When this irritating phenomenon is taking place on the spiritual level, I may need help in discerning. Someone farther along than I on the journey Home will help me to clarify and to discern.

Sometimes all that is needed is an attitude adjustment. Sometimes I just need to acknowledge and to celebrate the positive aspects of my life.

Sometimes I just need to be reminded that this life is not perfect. Sometimes, I have to face the fact that I have been concentrating on the negative to the extent of being unable to see God in the situation.

Fine-tuning is needed. Then the reception will be clear. Then I can take the next step.

The Wounded Plane

At a recent ecumenical gathering, someone mentioned that we may seem, at times, like a wounded airplane. We are up there, all right, but there is turbulence. We may become terrified and think that we will crash.

God is the pilot. We are not going to crash. We may be wounded, but God is our healer as well as our pilot. We will arrive on time. We will arrive safely.

Restore, Confirm, Strengthen, and Establish

These verbs jumped out at me yesterday as I pondered the first reading for Mass. They are from 1 Peter 5, 5-14. Over the course of the day, the four words kept coming back to me.

Then we watched the Inaugural Mass for Pope Benedict XVI. This passage from 1 Peter was proclaimed and again, I was very moved.

Restore. I can trust God to restore whatever has been taken from me. Whether it was my own carelessness, sin, the mistakes of others, whatever. God can still restore and renew. God can put everything back together. God can do anything

Confirm. God is with me and makes me firm. God validates me. God's work within me will one day be completed.

Strengthen. I do need new strength. God can build up my endurance and make me strong again.

Establish. God makes me stable. God settles me. God recognizes and accepts me. I am established.

Human Doors and Heaven's Doors

Doors open for you if you have the right connections! If you have a famous name, publishers are more willing to take a chance on your work.

If your parents went to such and such a university, the Admissions Office may give you preferential treatment. If you know someone famous and if you name drop, doors may open for you.

There are other doors. God's doors.

God has a different way of opening doors. God also has ways of closing doors. The Book of the Revelation mentions all sorts of doors.

It is God "… who opens and no one will shut, who shuts and no one opens (Revelation 3, 7 NRSV)."

What I want to do is to walk through each door God opens for me and to avoid like the plague every door God has closed.

"Look, I have set before you an open door, which no one is able to shut." (Revelation 3, 8 NRSV)

No door is closed to me if God decides to open that door. It is God who "… shatters the doors of bronze … " (Psalm 107,16 NRSV).

Stochastic Processes

Don't go there! I know that now.

We were new at Stanford and were at a gathering of graduate students in engineering. I have no idea where I ever heard the term "stochastic processes," but I decided to throw it into a conversation. Trying to look very wise, I asked if the researcher's work involved "stochastic processes."

BINGO! This person, whose work did indeed involve stochastic processes, talked on and on and on!

Fortunately my ignorance was never revealed. After listening to a long monologue about stochastic processes, I caught Terry's eye and pleaded silently for him to come and rescue me!

Catching a Few Rays

Springtime can still be cool. Every day with bright sunshine is welcome!

At the monastery, the rays of Jesus, Son of God and Son of Mary, are always there. Sitting in silence before the Blessed Sacrament brings calm and peace.

"And all of us, with unveiled faces, seeing the glory of the Lord as though reflected in a mirror, are being transformed into the same image from one degree of glory to another; for this comes from the Lord, the Spirit (2 Corinthians 3,18, (NRSV)."

It is not a matter of struggling to change myself. It is a matter of being in God's presence and allowing the holy rays to enter into me and to transform me.

Background Music

Yesterday, I was on a city street, taking the long way to a nearby town. Suddenly there was a blare of noise. The car in the next lane had its windows down, with very loud, raucous "music" blasting forth.

Glancing over, I saw the driver, a young woman, bouncing and grooving to the music. Then I noticed an infant in the back seat.

This was musical formation for the baby! Hopefully, the little one is also hearing lullabies, classical music, jazz, and other forms of music besides the kind of music that was being played that day.

What is the background music that is always playing in my life? My thoughts are always "playing," whether or not I am playing music of any kind.

Lately, my thoughts have been rather gloomy. Is it because of sorrow, health, the latest international crisis, or whatever? Maybe some of all the above and then some.

What I want to learn to do, more and more, is to try to think as St. Paul described. "Finally … whatever is true, whatever is honorable, whatever is just, whatever is pure, whatever is pleasing, whatever is commendable, if there is any excellence and if there is anything worthy of praise, think about these things (Philippians 4, 8 NRSV)."

It is a discipline to redirect my thoughts into healthier channels, but I want the background music, always "on," to be uplifting.

Ballerina in the Spirit

Feet again! After getting over the broken cuboid bone in my left foot, now the poor right foot is acting up again.

It was so beautiful to see the photographs of graceful ballerinas on the walls of the doctor's office. This doctor had treated the feet of many dancers and now they were dancing again.

A ballerina in the spirit! That's what I'd like to be.

Walking and leaping and praising God, as did the man at the Beautiful Gate of the Temple in Jerusalem is one my goals (Acts 3, 1-10).

The What Ifs

Back in Richardson, Texas, I was in a wonderful Bible study, led by a remarkable woman named Julie. Because I was in my twenties and

Julie was in her forties, I thought she was very wise, as well as very old!

Sometimes, I would tell Julie my list of "what ifs." What if this happens? What if that happens? I was a genius at thinking of so many negative possibilities.

Julie told me to ask myself, "What is the worst thing that could happen?" Then, she counseled me to think of reasons why it might not be so bad.

When I begin again on the "what ifs," I try to remember Julie's wise words and to refocus on God's love and provision for every single possibility.

Wait for the Tuna!

Francis the cat was bugging me at lunch, even though I knew he didn't like peanut butter and honey sandwiches. I stalled him, knowing that something better was in his future. Tuna!

For Francis, what could be better than tuna? Before making an old-fashioned tuna noodle casserole, I saved some tuna for Francis. He meowed loudly and came into the kitchen to devour his saucer of manna (tuna, in his case) from heaven.

God always has something better for us. We may howl for an appetizer, while God is preparing a feast for us. God waits, whether or not we wait with patience and with trust.

"For there is still a vision for the appointed time; it speaks of the end, and does not lie. If it seems to tarry, wait for it; it will surely come, it will not delay" (Habakkuk 2, 3 NRSV).

A Blueberry Muffin

Sometimes, I get tired of giving and giving and reaching out and reaching out. Although it is not reasonable to expect gratitude, it is still comforting.

What is the balance between reaching out to others and just saying, "Why bother?" We all wonder about that, sometimes.

When Christopher was in kindergarten, one day I baked fresh blueberry muffins for breakfast. Packing his lunch, I tucked in an extra muffin and told him to give one away.

He did. He offered the muffin to a little girl who threw it on the ground and said, "That's what I think of your muffin."

It is weary to go through life, believing that what we have to offer is thrown on the ground. Sometimes it is difficult to know when to give and when to withhold.

Jesus said to "... give, and it will be given to you (Luke 6, 38 NRSV)."

Jesus also said, "Do not give what is holy to dogs; and do not throw your pearls before swine, or they will trample them under foot and turn and maul you (Matthew 7, 6 NRSV)."

After acknowledging our very human frustration, we may return to the words of Jesus to "... love your enemies, do good, and lend, expecting nothing in return. Your reward will be great, and you will be children of the Most High; for he is kind to the ungrateful and the wicked. Be merciful just as your Father is merciful (Luke 6, 35, 36 NRSV)."

Sweet Pea!

What a surprise. The planter box where I had planted sweet peas had a brave bloomer. A strong, lonely sweet pea, a red one, had decided to bloom. All the rest of the sweet pea vines had long ago turned brown and seemingly lifeless.

Sun!

There is really not enough sun for us to grow sweet peas in that location. Still, I can't resist trying. It was supremely comforting to me this morning to see this little blossom.

Lost and Found

This is another form of grace that is truly amazing. Today, after searching and searching for my lost clip-on dark glasses, I found them!

Of all the places I never thought to look was in the clothes dryer. There they were, securely clipped on, actually in very good condition after having made a trip through the washer and dryer.

As with many of our prayers, the rejoicing is not so much in the answer, but in the sweet knowledge that the Lord is not too busy to answer even our little prayers.

I had been going through a stressful time and when I am stressed out, I tend to lose things. Finding the glasses was another way of reminding myself to slow down.

Baptismal Respect

When there are disagreements with other Christians, it is not always possible to have professional respect for the way in which the person is treating others. It is always possible, however, to have baptismal respect for that person.

Stretching the Mantle, Stretching the Prophet

I wonder how Elisha had to be "stretched" in order to assume Elijah's mantle.

God does indeed "stretch" us in many ways to prepare us for ministry.

The Medication Room

There is a little room, with a window in the door, in a nearby church. This is the room where the sacrament of reconciliation is celebrated.

One day, as I glanced at the sign, I misread the word "reconciliation." What I "saw" that day was the word "medication."

Maybe that's not so far off. There is great healing in this sacrament.

Geek Theologians

I was telling someone that, when I wrote the Gospel reflections, I was just writing and was not trying to be a deep theologian. The person laughingly asked if I'd said "geek" theologian!

Aromatic Composition

Looking on the back of a wonderfully fragrant bar of imported soap from Portugal, I saw the words, "aromatic composition." This accounted for only 2.5 per cent of the total composition of the soap and yet it was what one immediately noticed. Without this fragrance, the soap would have been merely a plain old bar of soap.

Sometimes, in this life, we feel so little and that maybe we don't count for much. If we are aspiring to offer our lives to God, we are a fragrance to God and to others. Our prayers are truly as sweet incense.

"Let my prayer be counted as incense before you, and the lifting up of my hands as an evening sacrifice (Psalm 141, 2 NRSV)."

In the Book of Revelation, the saints' prayers are referred to as golden bowls of incense (Revelation 5, 8).

St. Paul wrote of this fragrance to the Corinthians. "But thanks be to God, who in Christ always leads us in triumphal procession, and through us spreads in every place the fragrance that comes from knowing him (2 Corinthians 2, 14 NRSV)." The aromatic composition is there to give life!

Parking Problems

The problems of life often seem like parking places. As soon as one car, or as soon as the current problem, pulls out of the place, another is right there to pull in.

Yes, this too shall pass.

I am asking God to help me not to have such a crisis mentality, but rather to practice expecting good and receiving grace to deal with each situation.

Presence, Poustinia, Prophets and Potato Chips

(I can't remember what I was going to write about, but I like the alliterative title of what would have been this little essay and will just leave it).

A Message from the Pope

No, the Pope did not telephone me. I was in a really downcast state of mind when I saw a book of poetry on the shelf and idly opened it.

The author was young Karol Wojtyla. The poem had been written long ago, under a pseudonym.

Several lines from a particular poem jumped out at me. I read the lines over and over, They described exactly how I was feeling.

Later that afternoon, I took the book of poetry outside and read under the redwoods. The filtered sunlight, the breeze, and the silence all ministered to me.

One of the reasons the Psalms are so loved is because they describe in minute detail many, many states of mind. When we read these lines, we know we are understood.

The lines from the writings of the future Pope John Paul II also expressed deep feelings, with remarkable clarity and honesty. Others have felt the same way and were able to go on to live and to praise God.

That's what Karol did. l will, too. You will, too.

Where Do I Fit In?

Right there in the middle. I was feeling, not so much left out, but just in a puzzling place.

After a Mass in the home of friends, everyone was sitting around enjoying a little lunch. We were scattered all over the living room.

The little group to my left was mostly made of women discussing sewing. My knowledge of sewing consists in sewing on buttons. In middle school, I did manage to sew a dress, but my teacher was later committed to a mental institution. Just joking.

The group to my right consisted of several priests. There was some mention of a minor seminary college. Long ago, a priest we knew who had attended this college, had voiced his opinion. Smiling, he recalled, "It was like Alcatraz with daily Mass!" I ventured forth this quote, which was received with stunned silence, clearing of throats, and a change of topic.

Lord, where do I belong? Where do I fit in?

Cynthia, a clergy friend, answered this question for me years ago. We were in the Clinical Pastoral Education program at a large hospital. I confided to her, "I just don't fit in anywhere."

Cynthia had a very wise answer. She looked at me and said. "You fit in with Jesus."

What more could one wish?

The Down Time

No, this is not about computers. It is not about depression.

This is a different kind of "down." This is adoration. This is the time spent "down" at the feet of Jesus.

We may be driving on the freeway or folding laundry. We can instantly, in prayer, go "down" to the place of listening at the feet of Jesus.

This is where Mary of Bethany loved to be, when Jesus came to visit. Jesus came to visit his friends, Lazarus and his sisters, Martha and Mary, in their home at Bethany. Mary sat at the feet of Jesus and listened.

Jesus then lifts us from our "down" time to an "up" time. After being in prayer at his feet, he takes our hand and raises us. He leads us to a new place.

The down time is not wasted. It is time invested in the presence of Jesus. It is time which even now is bringing great dividends.

The Man Upstairs

Recently, I dreamed about someone who lived in an upstairs apartment. This apartment was accessible by an outside staircase.

Climbing up the stairs, I decided to visit the person who lived in this apartment. It was an old priest. He had a kindly face, shaggy hair, and a comfortable manner about him. The room was comfortably shabby and filled with an atmosphere of quiet peace and joy.

Immediately, I was at ease. It was easy to talk to this priest in an open, honest way about my concerns. I had no fears that I would be judged or condemned for the things that were troubling me. There was a deep, gentle wisdom about this priest.

I left after awhile, comforted by the knowledge that I could return. The old priest would be there. Jesus would be there.

Group Travel

Group travel. We travel as a group!

Francis, our marmalade cat, has certainly taught us this lesson. When he was younger, if he thought we were going to take a walk, he insisted on going with us. Even, at home, sometimes he wants to walk side by side with us, wherever we go.

The Israelites knew about group travel, also. Exodus 40 tell us about the cloud.

"For the cloud of the Lord was on the tabernacle by day, and fire was in the cloud by night, before the eyes of all the house of Israel at each stage of their journey (Exodus 40, 38, NRSV)." This is the last verse in the amazing book of Exodus.

How comforting that the guiding cloud was before the eyes of each and every person on the journey. How comforting that the guiding cloud was there at each and every part of the journey. God's presence was always there.

Whether or not we "feel" God's presence, God is truly present with us at every stage of our journey. We are not alone. We will "arrive" safely.

Wrapped in Words

When we view someone in a negative way and speak to that person and speak about that person in a negative way, we "wrap" them in these negative words.

They will become free and we will become free when we can practice wrapping them in a new way, by thinking and speaking only positive words to them and about them. This takes constant practice but the rewards are worth the effort.

LISTEN!

At the fish market today, I was behind a distinguished man wearing a yarmulke. He graciously invited me to go ahead, since I knew what I wanted. Salmon!

He commented about the rising price of fish. I was very preoccupied and just said that, even so, my husband and I really liked this fish market. Everything is absolutely fresh and is always without bones.

The market is in the same building with the seafood restaurant, so they're very careful about bones. It's never a good thing for a customer to find a bone.

So, I asked for the salmon, a half pound fillet, skin removed, complacently handed over a ten dollar bill and waited for a lot of change. The fish man handed me a few coins!

I had neglected to check the price of salmon. The price had almost doubled!

The moral -- listen! Listen to all those around you. They may have some very practical words of wisdom.

In the Wings Learning the Lines

Birds have wings. Theaters have wings. Does God have wings?

Psalm 91 has beautiful, comforting references to wings. It is under God's "wings" that we will find refuge (Psalm 91, 4).

I will rest, rest, in the shadow of God's wings. It is a place of growth.

In the wings of a theatre, we may grow impatient. We think we have learned our lines and are ready to go on stage. Maybe not. Not yet.

There are many ways of learning our lines. Lines memorized by the mind are one thing. Lines engraved on the heart are something else. The lines of life and destiny are learned in the wings. Boundary lines are learned in the wings.

The best lines are not the spoken lines. The best lines are the lines of silence.

Caution is learned in the wings. There is a time to go out on the stage and a time to stay hidden in the wings.

In the wings we may chafe and think nothing is happening. A lot is happening, however.

We are growing and developing and learning to practice. We are learning to learn to practice, to say, to love, and to live the lines God gives us. "The lines are fallen unto me in pleasant places... (Psalm 16, 6 KJV)."

Between a Rock and THE Rock

Between a rock and a hard place?

No, between a hard place and JESUS, THE ROCK.

A Table and THE Table

Competition extends even to the corner tables! My husband and I were going to our favorite fish and chips place one Friday evening

As he went to the counter to order, I went to find a table. Seeing an empty booth in the corner, I headed there and was about to sit down.

Whoosh! Not so fast!

I was intercepted by a woman who raced past me in the final few inches, grabbed the table, and smiled triumphantly.

Somehow, God gave me the grace to say, "Looks like we had the same idea. Please go ahead." She smiled and looked satisfied.

I found another table and just sat there, stunned and frankly angry at such rudeness. Earlier that morning, I had been to another Table where the manners were better.

The Table of the Lord. Mass. The Table of Jesus, the One who said he was among us as one who serves.

It's Time!

Waiting and waiting. We grow weary and wonder.

When will God show up? When will God's promise ever come to pass? We have waited so long.

When I was expecting Christopher, I remember being in the labor room, conscientiously trying to do the Lamaze exercises. I had prayed and waited so long for this child. Terry was a terrific labor coach.

When the pain begin to increase, I thought I couldn't go on. It was then that something really funny happened. The nurse came in, yelled out that it was "time" and I was hastily wheeled into the delivery room.

In the labor room, I had experienced as they say, some "discomfort." Now, I was getting really frightened about the pain that was ahead in the actual delivery.

As I was being wheeled into the delivery room, I announced that I had changed my mind about having a baby! I know that seems hilarious and I didn't really mean it. I had waited and prayed for so long for a child. It was just that, as the promise was about to be fulfilled, there was a last bout with labor.

It's not called labor for nothing. It takes work to deliver a baby.

87

It takes work on our part to see God's promises fulfilled. God requires our active cooperation.

This morning, my eyes landed on a verse that seems to apply to the birth of some of my writing projects. The verse is from Isaiah 37, 3. It refers to children about to be born, but to a lack of strength to bring them forth into the world.

Yes! That's how I've been feeling.

The books seem close to time of delivery, but I need a labor coach and some help in delivery. Terry does his part to encourage, but there's a part only I can do.

As with the birth of Christopher, I know God will provide. When it's God's time, the books will be born. Another ministry will also be born.

Grace and Mercy

In the midst of this difficult time with Francis, our cat, so sick, we had phone calls from Grace and Mercy. Such appropriate names!

Grace phoned first. She is a veterinary technician at the emergency pet hospital. She just phoned to check on how Francis was doing back at home. Then Mercy, also a vet tech, phoned a few days later.

Grace and Mercy! God sends us grace and mercy every day.

A Day of Glory!

You know those days when it seems that everything goes wrong?

Well, today was just the opposite. God knew I needed a day when everything went just swimmingly.

This is October 4, 2005, St. Francis' Day. We just brought Francis, our twenty year old golden marmalade cat, home from the animal hospital. He is truly the Comeback Cat.

On Sunday afternoon, we were basically planning to say goodbye to him. There seemed to be no hope he could recover and we did not want to do anything drastic to prolong his life.

Surprise! A few hours later, we were back at the hospital and he was sitting up. Yes!

The vet laughed, "The little pig! He just ate half a jar of baby food." After days of losing weight, not eating, and not responding to medicine, this was just amazing.

Earlier today, I had to go to my surgeon for a six month check-up. There was a parking place right in front of the office. The surgeon assured me that my condition was just fine.

I did several errands on the way home. It was just uncanny how I kept getting places to park right in front of the stores.

And then, the joy of picking up Francis at the animal hospital. Thank you, God. Thank you, all who have prayed for Francis. St. Francis of Assisi, St. Therese (the Little Flower), the Poor Clares, and so many others.

Solitude

The waters of creativity must be drawn from the well of solitude. Too much solitude, however, may lead to a sense of isolation.

Silence and solitude need be balanced with healthy interaction with others. The Holy Spirit will guide us in this matter.

Tourists

Someone jokingly said that some people don't go on their vacation while they are actually on their vacation. They are too busy documenting their vacation.

Too busy with cameras. Too busy with journals.

It is only after they return home that they enjoy their vacation. Seeing the pictures of where they had been. Reading the reflections and the notes they took while on their journey.

I'm feeling this way about the book of Gospel reflections I just completed. As I go back and make corrections, I read it as if for the first time. Insights hastily recorded now make sense. The Holy Spirit was, as always, ahead of me, showing me new vistas, knowing that later I would understand.

Framed!

Sitting alone and wondering why my day had been so difficult, I came to several conclusions. I need to frame each day with times of being consciously in God's presence. Yes, I am always in God's presence, but I still need moments of silence.

With all the noise and construction in the neighborhood, this is hard. There are cement mixers blocking the driveway, porta-potties, taco trucks, radios playing, etc. etc. etc. This goes on and on. As soon as one neighborhood project is finished, another begins. I drive away and have to navigate through streets crowded on both sides with more trucks, more taco trucks, more construction projects. Then, when I get to wherever I am going, I have to look and look for a place to park. This is hard.

Lord Jesus, please help me and show me how to live right here right now. Let me learn to be more aware of your shining presence.

I Do Windows, but I Don't Do 101

Limits. Boundaries.

I will. I won't.

You reach a point when you stop trying to be all things to all people. You cease to crave approval. You care, but you care about yourself in a new way.

Your "101" may not be the highway to which I refer. It may be a recipe you just don't want to make. It may be a committee meeting. It may be a lecture you don't want to present. It may be ….

Believing Without Seeing

BELIEVE!

After the resurrection of Jesus, Thomas was still having trouble believing it was really true. Could the crucified Christ really be alive again?

Thomas had not been present when the risen Jesus appeared to the disciples. It was so hard for him to believe.

Later, he was present when Jesus came to his followers. Jesus told Thomas to see his hands, to touch his side, and to believe. Thomas believed!

Jesus said that we are happy and blessed if we believe without seeing. This passage in the twentieth chapter of John's Gospel refers to the resurrection of Jesus.

What about us? Do we really believe in our own resurrection? Do we really believe that the power that raised Jesus from the dead will raise us to new life (Romans 8, 11)?

We may believe in our eventual resurrection after our death, but find it hard to believe in resurrection while still in this life. We may feel so depleted by circumstances that we find it difficult to believe life can ever be better.

Jesus invites us BELIEVE! Believe in the power of the risen Christ to restore us to life while we are still in this life.

BELIEVE!

To the Last Stone

The French city of St. Malo, destroyed in World War II, was later rebuilt, meticulously, to the very last stone.

Will not our loving God, who weeps when we suffer, also rebuild us?

Connect the Dots

Do you remember those connect the dot drawings? You proceed in numerical order to "connect the dots." When you have come to the last number, you have a complete drawing!

Sometimes we'd like to see the drawing before it's time. We get frustrated with the dots and don't see the connection between the various dots. The pattern seems to go in weird directions and we wonder if there will ever be a picture.

Maybe we should just concentrate on "living" the dots and let God do the connecting. Eventually, we'll see the picture which God had in mind all along.

A Portable Fan

What is God doing with my life? What is God doing in your life?

Sometime it seems nothing is happening. Are we making any difference as we seek to live for God?

The image that came to mind as I was musing in this way was of a little fan. The regular large kind is firmly attached to the ceiling.

This kind is different. It is little. It is portable.

It was as if God was reaching down from heaven and using us to refresh and to "fluff up" the environment in which we are currently placed.

Sometimes feathers get ruffled in this process. When God is through using us in a certain place, we are then sent on to another assignment.

The Rosies

A friend in our church told me about the sadness of her family in Texas. Their beloved pet dog, Rosie, had died.

We are in a time when our marmalade cat, Francis, is getting to be quite an elderly gentleman cat. He is so sweet and so loving and I am getting weepy just thinking of the time when he is not here with us.

My husband said I should have grown up on a farm, Then, perhaps, these matters wouldn't be so difficult. I'm not sure about that.

Rosie! I was reminded of another Rosie.

This was Rosie the Rat, who was a pet at our son's nursery school. The sad news came that Rosie the Rat had died.

The teacher, Mary, who actually did grow up on a farm, thought it would be good if the children were told about this in a straightforward way and that they actually saw Rosie's lifeless little body. So she showed them.

The next concern was about the class which would meet the next day. How could they see Rosie the Rat also?

Inspired, Mary put Rosie in the freezer! Actually, that was a good idea.

The only problem was that I never could open that freezer again. When it was my turn to help out at the school, I was happy to make the orange juice, serve the orange juice, and clean up afterwards. Opening the freezer and getting the frozen juice out, however, was not going to happen!

Prisoners

Lord, please release all prisoners of conscience, all prisoners of crime, and all prisoners of convenience. Lead us all to true freedom.

Tested on Animals

Many products have information on the back of the package stating that they are cruelty-free and that they have not been tested on animals. I always look for this information.

Advances in veterinary care has been remarkable. Micro-chips, dental care, vaccinations, etc. etc.

Prayer is another way of caring for animals. I have been praying for several animals, the pets of friends. They are very important in the lives of their families.

Francis, the marmalade Gospel-cat, has received the prayers of many. With great joy and gratitude, I have watched as he has recovered.

Praying for difficult situations is a real challenge. If we have had a time of discouragement or despair, we may tend to give up on prayer. We may even think we have given up on God or that God has given up on us.

This is not so. God finds very creative ways to come to us and to reassure us. Our prayers for ourselves, for other people, and even for animals, are all held close to the heart of God. They will be answered in the way that is the very best for all concerned.

Root Canal of the Soul

Pain. Treatment. Peace

The dentist removes what is not good from our tooth. The tooth

94

is then able to be a tooth again. The hardest part, during this procedure, for me, is simply to stay still. I can't fix this tooth. That is the dentist's job.

Lord Jesus, help me to stay still while you do the work of restoring my soul (Psalm 23, 3).

Where Are You?

Once, in the chapel of the Immaculate Heart Monastery of the Poor Clares, I was in a state of great discouragement. I asked God, "Where ARE you?"

God answered, deep within my heart. I seemed to hear God respond, "That is not the right question. The right question is to ask where you, Janis, are. The answer is that you are in My Sacred Heart."

God's Guppy

Although I may not be where I want to be or where I think I should be, at this stage of my like, still I trust in the Lord's wisdom and love.

I'd rather be a little guppy for God in the right ocean, than be a big shark in the wrong pond.

The words of the Psalmist came to mind. "For a day in your courts is better than a thousand elsewhere. I would rather be a doorkeeper in the house of my God than live in the tents of wickedness (Psalm 84, 10 NRSV)."

The Three R's

Resolution. Restoration. Redemption.

Resolution. Resolution may not occur in the way we wish.

Restoration. Restoration may be delayed.

Redemption. Redemption, however, is certain.

As we continue actively to trust God and do the work we are called to do, all will be resolved, restored, and redeemed.

Whiners or Winners

Don't you get sick of people who keep whining about how hard life is? So and so did such and such to them.

Poor babies. All they can do is cry and whine.

I have been that way. Perhaps, you have, too. Been there, done that!

Instead of denying that we have been jerks, we need to be honest with ourselves. By talking about our problems all the time, we have become idolaters.

We have made idols out of our problems. We have become so focused on ourselves and our problems that we have left God out of the equation.

What is the equation? The equation is that with God, I am a winner. You are a winner.

We win because we have invited God to come into the troublesome situation. Only God can either straighten out the crazy, mixed-up mess or else come up with a solution that we could never have dreamed up on our own.

Lord Jesus, help me and forgive me. I think I've turned a situation over to you and then I start rehearsing it all over again and then start to feel sorry for myself. You have called us to be winners. You have assured us of your constant love and protection. We are safe with you. Let this be a fresh new day of looking to you and rejoicing that you are calling us to a new place of freedom.

Don't Skip

If you have ever read aloud to children, you know that they know every single word of a particularly beloved story. If you are tired or in a hurry and skip a few words in the story, the child will let you know!

God wants us to tell the whole story. We don't have to be concerned that God is tired or bored or in a hurry.

The sovereign God of the whole universe is waiting for us. We are invited to pour out the whole story, all our fears, and all our concerns. We will be given loving attention and assurance that God knows and understands what is really bothering us and how to help us.

Suffering and Singing

The Book of Job is placed before the Psalms in the Hebrew Scriptures. When we think of Job, we instantly think of suffering. When we think of the Psalms, we remember that the very word "psalms" means "songs."

God invites to be very real in expressing our emotions. All our emotions. If we are stuck in suffering, it helps to remember that singing will follow.

Relating or Writing?

Well, of course it's both. I realized, however, yesterday morning, that I had my priorities out of order.

My morning routine is to take a cup of coffee and immediately, after prayer, begin to write the daily Scripture reflection. The Bible and notebook are always in the same place.

Not yesterday morning! No Bible anywhere! I realized then that I had become, once again, putting the work of the Lord before the Lord of the work.

What did I think would happen, anyway? Did I think the Lord was engaged in celestial hand-wringing?

The Bible, of course, was located, in my study by the computer, and the reflection was written. I learned that I need to cool it a bit and relax.

Miss OK

She meant well, even if her vocabulary was limited. She was working in a Chinese restaurant as a waitress and no matter what you asked, she replied, "OK."

Initially irritated, I later realized God had something for me to learn here. Sometimes it's just easier to say "OK."

Moses and Manna

Gripe. Gripe. Gripe.

Moses. Manna.

The Israelites were getting sick and tired of God's servant Moses and of God's provision, manna.

We do this too. We don't like what others are doing. We don't like whatever is the manna in our lives.

Lord Jesus, forgive us. You know we act this way. You know what manna is best for us at this time. Help us to make the best of what you have provided for us. We praise you for your presence with us and thank you for your provision.

The Hamburger Angels

We were on the way for a few peaceful days at the ocean. The ritual called for a stop for a hamburger at about half way. It's always a crazy, hectic place, but fun.

For some reason, I was feeling a little weary and wasn't sure about braving the hamburger crowds. It' s hard to get a place to sit. People watch like vultures for an empty table. As the previous diners show signs of leaving, the vultures gather, prepared to swoop.

We were at a small table very close to a group of three Asian men who were traveling for business in America. They quizzed us about the popularity of this little hamburger place. The bigger place, with the more famous name, was not nearly as crowded as this one.

We talked hamburgers, travel, and even God came into the conversation. I believe that these three were God's messengers, God's hamburger angels, to cheer me up and lighten the way.

"Followship"

Follow God. Fellowship will follow.

Fellowship with God and with others. There will be delightful new open doors through which we will walk.

The Mysteries of YOU!

As we pray the rosary, the Holy Spirit is transforming us. As we meditate on the joyful, luminous, sorrowful, and glorious mysteries in the life of our Lord, we ourselves are being transformed.

Little by little, the mysteries of our own lives are illumined and transformed for the Lord's purposes. Little by little.

The Blue Army and Earplugs

It was at the Eight Day Silent Retreat in the summer of 2003. The lady next door was a world class snorer and I was becoming incoherent from lack of sleep. There was nowhere else to move to, as the retreat house was filled for the retreats.

I left the retreat house to go to a pharmacy to buy earplugs. I had called my husband about this sleep dilemma and he met me at the store. A really romantic date -- shopping for earplugs!

A lady who worked at the store was showing me the different kinds of earplugs and asking me about the retreat. She became quite excited about the retreat and wanted to recruit me for the Blue Army.

After some time, I left the store, returned to the retreat and tried the earplugs. They didn't work. Still, there were many graces from the retreat.

Cat Food in My Sandals!

It was early morning when I went into the kitchen, poured orange juice, and started coffee. Francis, the marmalade Gospel-cat, would be along soon and I was trying to get his cat food all ready. He usually had dry food, but, once in a while, had wet food as a treat.

Something cold and wet seemed to hit my foot and land on the floor. Cat food!

Francis came and started to eat from the floor as I cleaned the bit of food from my foot. He took this change of dining etiquette in stride, although I redirected him to the laundry room where his cat food was properly in the bowl.

I have learned so much from this now quite elderly feline friend. Instead of fussing at me that I had dropped his food on the floor, he simply took it as it was, where it was.

Levels of Trust

If you feel you are being stretched almost beyond endurance in your call to trust God, please try to be patient and take heart.

Your reward will be greater, because your level of trust has had to go deeper. The time of stretching will not always be this intense.

This time is terribly difficult, but it will not last forever, The joy to come will last forever. Alleluia!

Hanging Out with the Wrong Crowd?

If the people around you seem to drag you down, maybe you're hanging out with the wrong people. They are full of doom and gloom. They seem always under a dark cloud.

Another crowd. Another cloud.

There really is another crowd and another cloud.

Hebrews 12, 1 tells us of the great cloud of witnesses, those who have completed their earthly journey and are now cheering us on as we continue. Jesus and Mary and the angels and the saints are here to lift us, to pray for us, and to bring us joy and hope.

When Will This Baby Ever Be Born?

What kind of physician do you see when you are going to have a baby? An obstetrician (an "OB"), course!

God is trying to bring something to birth through our lives. How do we cooperate with our wise, loving Physician?

We can practice our own form of "OB."

Obedience. Boldness.

Obedience. Obedience to God leads to freedom, a freedom unimaginable.

Boldness. This new freedom in God will lead us to live boldly, with a radical trust in God.

At the right time, our Divine "OB" will bring us to the delivery room for the birth. The labor has been long and difficult, but the birth is imminent. This birth will be worth the wait!

Mother's Robe

My mother had a lovely, long, flowered, silk robe. Light. Delicate. So graceful and lovely. After Mother died, I kept the robe and even occasionally wore it.

One day, as I was about to visit my neighbor, Elizabeth, who was in the Sunrise community, I felt led to take the robe with me. Someone there might enjoy it.

Elizabeth, nearly 100, is much beloved and has many visitors. Maybe there was someone else at the Sunrise who was not so privileged.

At the desk, somewhat hesitantly, I brought out the robe and asked if any of the residents might enjoy this robe. The young woman's face broke into a smile. She assured me that she knew the very person. It was an older lady who was there, very unhappy and very depressed, She would give the robe to her.

I left, feeling so happy. The robe with its delicate blooms would bring cheer, I hoped, to this lady.

Lifted into God's Presence

It was a Sunday morning, when I was sitting on the sofa and enjoying a cup of coffee. Francis, our quite elderly marmalade cat, had tried his best to jump up to sit beside me as is his custom. He paced back and forth, trying, without success, to jump and get up on the sofa.

In the past, I had been very strict about not letting him be on the sofa. Now, I was just glad he was alive and was able to jump a little.

"That's ok, old guy," I said to him. I'll lift you." I reached down and lifted him up to be with me.

"You're here," I said to him. He purred, so happy to have reached his destination.

I think that when I'm too tired to go on, God will gently reach down, lift me up and say, "You're here. You're Home."

Joyce at the Monastery

I was about to go to the monastery for a little peace and quiet during this last round of noisy construction in our neighborhood. Maybe that is not the highest motive, but the Lord takes us as we are.

Then, I remembered an invitation I wanted to hand deliver to someone who worked a few miles away. So, I dropped off the invitation, and then proceeded to the monastery.

Peace at last! Only a few minutes was better than nothing.

Silence. Then, it was time to go.

I heard the front door of the monastery open as I was getting ready to go. Walking toward the door, I stopped.

Joyce! What a lovely surprise! We had been in a prayer group back in the 1980's.

As she explained, she was about to go to Mass, but remembered to stop at the monastery. She had left her cell phone somewhere, and decided to check several places.

She didn't find it at the monastery, but I was so grateful for God's timing. One minute earlier or later and I would have missed her. I left the monastery, marveling at God's sense of perfect timing in our lives.

Lemon Verbena and the Bonnie Madonna

Out in our herb garden, there is a lemon verbena plant. Actually, it's more of a bush! There are wonderfully fragrant leaves which are easy to dry and to leave in bowls for potpourri or to tie into fragrant little sachets.

Early in the summer, I cut a sprig of this verbena and brought it inside to live in a little vase near the crystal Madonna.

This is a lovely Madonna that my friend Bonnie gave me when I graduated from the seminary. The Madonna is on our kitchen window sill.

Other times, when I have cut the lemon verbena and brought it inside to place in vases, it looked nice for a few days and then began to wither. Not this time.

This lemon verbena sprouted roots and filled up the vase. The leaves did not wither this time.

More and more roots! I have now transferred the plant, still in water, to a larger glass.

This has been such a comfort to me and I hope the story will also be a comfort to Bonnie when I tell her. Earlier in the spring, her father died. I wrote a note, but will now tell her about the lemon verbena.

We will stay close to Mary, the Madonna, the mother of Jesus. She calls us to stay close to her son. She tells us to listen to Jesus and to do whatever Jesus tells us to do (John 2, 5). Rooted in Jesus and close to Mary, we will grow strong and will blossom and flourish.

The Right Place

It was early morning and I was having my coffee and writing scripture reflections. Francis, our elderly marmalade cat, was standing nearby. He was near the sofa, but under the coffee table.

Francis knows it is too hard for him to jump on the sofa to be near me. Usually, I just scoop him up and place him beside me.

Today, though, he was in a place where it was hard for me to reach him. After awhile, he moved to another place. This made it a lot easier for me to pick him up and to place him on the sofa, where he began to purr contentedly.

Although God has all power and can find us and place us anywhere at all, we do have some say in the matter. We have choices to think and to speak and to act in ways that please God. It is then easier for God to reach us and easier for us to be found. We are in a better position for God to reach us and to place us where we belong.

Perry Mason

In these days of answering machines, cells phones, and the option of call waiting, we forget about how we used to use the telephone. If the phone rang, someone answered it.

Except for Kathey's mother! Kathey and I were college friends and her mother was a devoted fan of the old "Perry Mason" television programs.

If someone phoned during this program, she did not ignore the call. Nor did she spend time on it.

She would pick up the phone, say "Perry Mason!" and then hang up. The caller learned not to call during "Perry Mason."

The Lord is calling us all the time. We don't have to say "Perry Mason" if we don't want to talk with the Lord. We are free to be honest and tell the Lord what is bothering us. The Lord is longing for us to be real. The Lord is longing to free us to live in joy.

Invisible Ink

Jesus is writing his message on our life. We can't see it. We can't read it.

Later, we will see. Others will see. All will become clear.

Response and Effect

Sometimes we really and truly believe we are to say or to do a certain thing. Maybe it's simple, such as a making a phone call or writing a note.

We follow through and make the call or write the note. What happens then? It may appear that nothing has happened.

Just because there was no response does not mean that what we did was without effect. We continue to follow God, trusting that whatever we did that was truly inspired by God will have the effect God desires.

Violets!

I had walked by this house every spring and enjoyed the beauty and the fragrance of the delicate purple violets, planted between the sidewalk and the street. Then, for whatever reason, I did not walk down that street for quite a while.

When I eventually did walk by the "violets" house, I was very sad. The violets were gone. Where they had grown, now there were bricks covering the ground.

It seems like life does that to our dreams. It seems that what was fragrant and beautiful was removed and destroyed, replaced by "bricks."

Somehow and somewhere I do believe God will give complete restoration. The violets will be bloom again.

Plastic Surgery for a Butterfly

Years ago, I thought that a long-awaited promise from God was about to be fulfilled. Everything was falling into place.

I was so happy. At last!

My spiritual director, at the time, was also happy for me and even told me that I seemed to be like a butterfly, at long last emerging from the chrysalis. It was a wonderful time.

Then, at the last minute, everything seemed to be snatched away. I felt that, just as I had barely emerged as a butterfly, my wings were ripped off and I could not fly. I could not even live.

Years went by. At a retreat, I told this story to another retreatant. She told me that God could even perform spiritual "plastic surgery" on butterflies. One day, I will be free to fly where God wants me to fly.

The Resurrected Robin

CRASH! I was startled as I heard a terrific thud against the front window. What was this?

Running to look, I saw what appeared to be a very dead robin in the front yard.

For years, I have had had a horror of dead birds. It is so hard for me to see these beautiful creatures, designed by their Creator to be soaring freely in the skies, to be lying dead on sidewalks or on streets. I cannot bear to look.

It was in late afternoon, in late winter, when this happened. Wild thoughts of calling the vet or the animal rescue people raced through my mind.

Instead, I was transfixed by the front window. Steeling myself to look steadily upon this immobile creature whose eyes seemed to stare through me, I began to pray. I prayed for the life of Christ and the light of Christ to come into this little creature. Nothing. No movement. Nothing.

I stood there and prayed. Nothing.

I stood immobile, myself, and kept praying. I don't remember all the exact words, except for asking for the light of Christ and the life of Christ to come into this robin.

Closing my eyes briefly and looking away for an instant, I was startled to observe the robin. The robin was now standing! Not moving a bit, but at least standing.

I continued to pray. Over the course of half an hour, perhaps, there began to be slight changes. The robin's head began to turn, ever so slowly, from side to side.

No longer able to bear this alone, I stepped to my purse and retrieved my cell phone. I did not want to go to the kitchen phone and be unable to see the little robin.

Still standing by the window, where I could observe the robin, I phoned an understanding friend. She listened to me and prayed along with me.

Wonderfully and gloriously, eventually, the robin flew! Up and up into the branches of the sycamore tree. And then away into the sky.

A Piece of Chalk

This is early fall, when students of all ages go back to school. The scent of crayons is so much part of our memories of our early school days. There is even a new cologne that is supposed to have the fragrance of crayons.

There is very little noise when we draw with a crayon. The crayon is soft and colorful. It produces a lovely color with very little noise or disturbance to those who may be nearby.

A piece of chalk, however, is different. Unlike the crayon, it does produce noise when it is used to write on a chalkboard. Sometimes, the noise it produces is exceedingly unpleasant. Screechy!

God sends us messages written with various instruments. When the instrument is sweet and soft, like a crayon, it's easy to listen to God's message.

When the instrument is a piece of chalk and the message hurts our ears and our souls, it is harder to listen. We want to put our hands over our ears or to run away.

As hard as it is to listen to a message written in a blunt, screechy manner, it is even harder to be the piece of chalk. It is hard to be used of God to deliver a message which is unpopular.

Perhaps prophets are like that piece of chalk. They often deliver messages which challenge us. They may deliver messages which anger us.

Often, prophets don't even know that God is using them. They just know that they are trying to live for God.

Impossible?

It was January 18, 2012, the first day of the Week of Prayer for Christian Unity. This week is very important to me because the unity of the church is very important to me.

Jesus prayed to his Father, "I ask not only on behalf of these [the first disciples], but also on behalf of those who will believe in me though their word, that they may all be one. As you, Father, are in me and I am in you, may they also be in us, so that the world may believe that you have sent me (John 17, 20-21 NRSV)."

Jesus said, "I am the good shepherd. I know my own and my own know me, just as the Father knows me and I know the Father. And I lay down my life for the sheep. I have other sheep that do not belong to this fold. I must bring them also, and they will listen to my voice. So there will be one flock, one shepherd (John 10, 14-16 NRSV)."

In his April 20, 2005, address, to the Cardinals, Pope Benedict XVI emphasized his "… primary commitment … of working tirelessly toward the reconstitution of the full and visible unity of all Christ's followers."

So, back to January 18, 2012. I was shopping in a spice store, looking for various blends of spices and herbs. Very discouraged over a number of matters which seemed "impossible" of solution, I realized that the music being piped in was from the musical, "The Man of La Mancha." The song currently being played was "The Impossible Dream."

I was very moved by the Lord's tenderness in reassuring me that the matters troubling me, including Christian unity, are by no means impossible. "For nothing will be impossible with God (Luke 1, 37, NRSV)."

Oil at the Carwash

Car wash? I had no intention of going to the car wash that morning.

I was at a stationer's store and had planned to stop a friend's house in a nearby city. Still, I felt strongly led to go to this particular car wash.

So, off to the car wash! After indicating that I only wanted the five-minute exterior wash, I paid and took my cup of coffee to a bench outside to wait.

Crash! Crunch! Cries!

A vehicle emerging from the carwash had somehow gone out of control and had crashed into a small red car which was now crumpled. In between, lying on the ground, was a young man.

Everything went into slow motion. I slowly set the coffee down and walked toward the small group of people gathered around the injured man, now silent, who was lying on the ground.

Someone was calling 911. Police were on the way. An ambulance was on the way

Remembering I had a small vial of blessed healing oil from the

Jesuit Retreat House in my purse, I walked over to the young man on the ground, anointed him, praying very quietly and very quickly.

The paramedics then arrived and took him to the hospital. Several other people and I were asked to give statements to the police.

The next day, I phoned the car wash and asked the condition of the man who had been injured. He was alive!

All that happened was that his knee was badly injured. Surgeries lay ahead of him, but he was ALIVE. Thanks be to God.

Double Dipping

No, this is not about the distressing habit of dipping twice in the guacamole or whatever with the same cracker or carrot. This is a GOOD kind of double dipping

Years ago, before I became a Catholic, I had heard about offering our suffering to the Lord for his purposes. Rather timidly, I started to try to do this.

The Lord is so merciful and guided me gently. I was overwhelmed by how the Lord began answering my prayers on behalf of others.

So I prayed and wondered. Is there a way to "recycle" or to "double dip?"

This Lent I am offering the same sufferings but for yet another purpose. Interesting prayer experiment, if nothing else.

Aqua/Black Times Three

Only the Lord could have pulled this off! I was planning a big garden party for Terry's birthday. We were even having a jazz combo.

Who could help us? The day before the party, we went to a Saturday Vigil Mass and saw several students from the Youth Group people. Aha!

Two of them, a high school girl and boy, agreed to help. They would arrive at our house early on the afternoon of the party.

I was very relieved, but wanted one more helper. I phoned a friend and her teenage daughter graciously agreed to come and help.

The first two arrived together and were dressed in aqua shirts and black Bermuda shorts. Very spiffy.

Then the third helper arrived, not knowing about the other two. She also was dressed in an aqua shirt and black Bermuda shorts. It was as if God sent us a very special team, even color-coordinated!

"Stay the Course, Lassie"

Discouraged and exhausted, I asked myself a question. How would two Scottish heroes in the faith encourage me? Their lives had been of great inspiration to me for a very long time.

The two Scots. They were already "there," in the "great cloud of witnesses" described in Hebrews 12, 1.

The Rev. Dr. Peter Marshall (A Man Called Peter), who served as Chaplain of the United States Senate.

Eric Liddell, the Olympic runner, whose story was told in the film "Chariots of Fire".

In the film, "Chariots of Fire," Eric compares faith to running in a race. "I have no formula for winning the race. Everyone runs in her own way, or his own way. And where does the power come from, to see the race to its end? From within. If you commit yourself to the love of Christ, then that is how you run a straight race."

What would the Scots tell me? As I prayed, I think what they would say to me is, "Stay the course, lassie."

"Therefore, since we are surrounded by so great a cloud of witnesses, let us also lay aside every weight and the sin that clings so closely, and let us run with perseverance the race that is set before us, looking to Jesus the pioneer and perfector of our faith, who for the sake of the joy that was set before him endured the cross, disregarding its shame, and has taken his seat at the right hand of the throne of God (Hebrews 12, 1-2 NRSV)."

"Invisible"

One of my favorite parts in the film "Princess Diaries," is when the young teenager, Michael, who worked in a garage, asked Princess Mia why she had chosen him as her escort for the ball.

Michael asked, "Why me?!

Princes Mia answered, "Because you saw me when I was invisible."

"Heart Speaks to Heart"

Very perplexed about a particular situation, I prayed and felt led to read something originally written by Albino Luciani (Pope John Paul I) in Illustrissima and later quoted in The Smiling Pope.

In his "letter" to Saint Therese of Lisieux, "Joy, Exquisite Charity," he wrote, quoting Archbishop Perini, that "... there are not many loves, but only one ...."

For the situation I had been concerned with, this made perfect sense to my heart as well as to my mind.

I was further illumined by something Joseph Ratzinger (Pope Benedict XVI) wrote in Daughter Zion in 1983. The future Pope wrote, "... there is a pure answer and ... God's love finds its irrevocable place within it ...."

"Heart speaks to heart." This was the motto of Cardinal Newman.

At Cardinal Newman's beatification Mass on September 20, 2010, Pope Benedict XVI referred to this motto: "Cardinal Newman's motto, 'Cor ad cor loquitur,' or 'Heart speaks unto heart,' gives us an insight into his understanding of the Christian life as a call to holiness, experienced as the profound desire of the human heart to enter into intimate communion with the Heart of God."

My New Nest

"As the marsh hen secretly builds on the watery sod,
     Behold I will build me a nest on the greatness of God:
     I will fly in the greatness of God …."

from "The Marshes of Glynn,"
a poem by Sydney Lanier

A.M.D.G.

You may order additional copies of this book

from www.amazon.com, www.barnesandnoble.com,

or through your favorite bookstore.

Printed in the USA
CPSIA information can be obtained
at www.ICGtesting.com
JSHW022345141023
49997JS00001B/48